欧洲福利国家“集成式老年政策”与潜在贫困问题研究

——汉、英

徐 佳 著

中国商务出版社
CHINA COMMERCE AND TRADE PRESS

图书在版编目(CIP)数据

欧洲福利国家"集成式老年政策"与潜在贫困问题研究 : 汉、英 / 徐佳著. --北京 : 中国商务出版社, 2019.9

ISBN 978-7-5103-3071-1

Ⅰ. ①欧… Ⅱ. ①徐… Ⅲ. ①老年人—贫困问题—社会政策—研究—欧洲—汉、英 Ⅳ. ①F150.6

中国版本图书馆 CIP 数据核字(2019)第 207990 号

欧洲福利国家"集成式老年政策"与潜在贫困问题研究
OUZHOU FULI GUOJIA JICHENG SHI LAONIAN ZHENGCE YU QIANZAI PINKUN WENTI YANJIU
徐 佳 著

出　　版:中国商务出版社有限公司
地　　址:北京市东城区安定门外大街东后巷 28 号　　邮　　编:100710
责任部门:职业教育事业部(010-64218072　295402859@qq.com)
责任编辑:魏　红

总 发 行:中国商务出版社发行部(010-64208388　64515150)
网　　址:http://www.cctpress.com
邮　　箱:cctp@cctpress.com

排　　版:北京亚吉飞数码科技有限公司
印　　刷:北京亚吉飞数码科技有限公司
开　　本:787 毫米×1092 毫米　1/16
印　　张:11.5　　字　　数:149 千字
版　　次:2021 年 1 月第 1 版　　印　　次:2021 年 1 月第 1 次印刷
书　　号:ISBN 978-7-5103-3071-1
定　　价:60.00 元

Chairman: Prof. Dr. Kai-Uwe Schnapp

First supervisor: Prof. Dr. rer. pol. Birgit Pfau-Effinger

Second supervisor: Prof. em. Dr. Rolf von Lüde

Date of disputation: October 30, 2018

Abstract

The main research question of this dissertation is how ageing policy differ in their hypothetical impact on poverty risk of older people in European welfare states.

In comparative welfare state research, the ways in which welfare state policy frame poverty and social inequality for senior citizens is an important issue. Various empirical studies that usually focus on a single policy field have analysed the role of welfare state policies for social inequality and poverty in old age. These policy fields mainly include pension policies (Carrera et al., 2011; Foster, 2011; Grech, 2014) and long-term care policies (Waldhausen, 2014; Huber Zoólyomi, 2012; Leichsenring, Billings, Nies, 2013; Speer & Pryor, 2014). However, such approaches overlook the fact that different policy fields interact in their role in terms of the income situation of people in old age. It is important to analyze how the different policy fields interact in their framing of social inequality and poverty risk of older people.

A theoretical approach of "ageing policy" is introduced in this dissertation. This approach is based on the interaction of three policy fields in the ways in which they are framing social inequality and poverty of older people. Besides policies regarding pension and long-term care, it also includes social assistance policy. It is argued that all three types of policies are highly relevant in their role with regard to the risk of poverty in old age. In addition, I also introduce an "ideal-typical" typology of different types of ageing policy that are based on different ways in which ageing policy hypothetically impact on poverty risk for older people. Based on this theoretical framework, I develop the main hypotheses of the study.

In the empirical part of this dissertation, I introduce the findings of a cross-national comparative study on the hypothetical impact of different types of ageing policies on the poverty risk of senior citizens in European welfare states. This dissertation examines the ageing policy of Germany, Denmark and the UK by looking at the institutional level. The interaction of ageing policy is analyzed by their generosity and the hypothetical impact on preventing poverty risk for older people. This dissertation also analyzes how each ageing policy field compensates with each other.

The dissertation can make an innovative contribution to comparative welfare state research and analysis of poverty risks in old age. It offers a new, complex theoretical typology for comparative analysis about the role of welfare state policies for poverty of senior citizens. This dissertation makes direct measurement of the role of policies for poverty at the institutional level. It is a new type of measurement of the social policies.

摘 要

本文的主要研究问题是欧洲福利国家的“集成式老年政策”对老年群体潜在贫困风险的影响，以及“集成式老年政策”体系中多种政策之间的作用关系。

在福利国家比较研究中，福利国家政策如何作用于老年群体贫困问题及社会不平等问题是一个重要的议题。通常相关研究只针对单一的社会政策领域对于老年贫困问题的影响，这些政策领域主要包括养老金政策（Carrera et al.，2011；Foster，2011；Grech，2014）和长期护理政策（Waldhausen，2014；Huber Zoólyomi，2012；Leichsenring，Billings，Nies，2013；Speer & Pryor，2014）。然而，这些已有的研究忽视了这样一个事实，即不同的政策领域在老年群体收入状况方面存在着相互作用关系，分析不同政策领域如何在相互作用的情况下影响老年群体贫困风险十分重要。

本文提出了一个理论概念：“集成式老年政策”。这个概念的提出基于社会政策的三个政策体系，即养老金政策体系、长期护理政策体系和社会救助政策体系对于老年群体贫困风险的作用关系。本文认为这三类政策体系在共同作用于老年群体潜在贫困风险方面直接密切相关。因此，文中提出了针对于欧洲不同类型的“集成式老年政策”的理论分类。基于以上理论框架，文中提出了相应的研究假设。

在实证部分，本文介绍了不同欧洲福利国家多种类型的“集成式老年政策”对老年群体潜在贫困问题影响的国际比较研究。实证部分选取了德国、丹麦和英国的“集成式老年政策”，并且对于政策的分析全部基于国家政策制度层面。"集成式老年政策"每个政策领域的分析和政策整合研究均基于政策的慷慨程度及其对老年群体潜在贫困的影响。本文还分析了"集成式老年政策"每个政策领域的内在作用关系。

本文可以为福利国家比较研究和老年贫困问题研究做出贡献。文中针对福利国家政策体系和老年群体潜在贫困问题的关系研究提出了一个新的、复杂的理论分类。本文从国家制度层面,将社会政策在贫困问题上所起的作用进行了直接的测量,同时提出了一种对政策及政策慷慨程度进行直接测量的方法。

Contents

目　录

List of abbreviations

AROP	at the risk of poverty
DG EMPL	the European Commission
EAPN	European Anti-Poverty Network
Eurostat	Statistical Office of the EU
EU	the European Union
EU-SILC	the European Union Survey of Income and Living Conditions
GNI	Gross National Income
ILC	the International Longevity Centre
JRF	the Joseph Rowntree Foundation
MEB	the Minimum Essential Budgets
MIS	the Minimum Income Standards
MPI	multidimensional poverty index
OECD	the Organization for Economic Co-operation and Development
PPP	purchasing power parities
PCE	personal consumption expenditure
SAMN	the System of Assistance in Material Need
SPC	Social Protection Committee
SSPTW	Social Security Programs Throughout the World
UNDP	United Nations Development Program

Chapter 1 Introduction

Aging and poverty risk for older people are two of the major issues in our social world.

In comparative welfare state research, the ways in which welfare state policy are framing social inequality of senior citizens is an important issue. Different research fields that usually focus on a single policy field have analyzed the role of welfare state policies for social inequality and poverty in old age. These policy fields mainly include pension policies (Carrera et al., 2011; Foster, 2011; Grech, 2014) and long-term care policies (Waldhausen, 2014; Leichsenring et al., 2013; Speer & Pryor, 2014). However, such approaches overlook the fact that different policy fields interact in their role in terms of the income situation of people in old age. It is therefore important to analyze how the different policy fields interact in their framing of social inequality and poverty risk of older people.

This dissertation aims to answer the question: how do aging policies differ in their impact hypothetically on the poverty risk of older people in European welfare states.

This dissertation introduces a new theoretical approach to the analysis of the role of welfare state policies for poverty in old age, which is defined here as concept of "ageing policy". It is based on the combination and interaction of three different policy fields which have strict relevance to older people's life condition and poverty risks, pension policy, long-term care policy and social assistance policy. Pension, long-term care and social assistance policies interact in their influence on the risk of poverty for older people and on their life situation. However, to some degree, both pension and long-term care policy fields can be designed for social and economic development reasons so that they do not avoid poverty for older people by themselves. In that case, social assistance policies may fill the gap. This "ageing policy" shows different characteristics and different degrees of impact on older people's poverty condition in different countries. I introduce a new "ideal-typical" typology that comprises different types of ageing policy, which offers an adequate theoretical framework for comparative analysis of ageing policy. This dissertation then uses this theoretical typology for comparative analysis of the role of ageing policy for poverty risk of senior citizens among countries in European welfare states. This dissertation analyses how ageing policy interacts in the different types of welfare states. It looks at whether such policies reduce or increase poverty among senior citizens, and how far they leave gaps for poverty risk for them and compares these gaps with national poverty thresholds.

The main assumption of this dissertation is that different types of ageing policies differ in their impacts on avoiding poverty risk for older people in European welfare states.

The definition of poverty in this dissertation, on the one hand, follows a European Council decision of 1984 which was on the target to combat poverty, as:

The poor shall be taken to mean persons, families and groups of persons whose resources (material, cultural and social) are so limited as to exclude them from the minimum acceptable way of life in the Member state in which they live (*EEC*, 1985, *p*. 24-25).

On the other hand, it is also based on the definition of European Union and thresholds recommended by the Statistic Office of the EU (Eurostat), in this dissertation, the definition of poverty only focuses on older people. However, this definition is not the same as real poverty in reality, because, older people have multiple income sources, i. e. pensions, capital assets, relative supports, social benefits, earnings, public assistance, veteran's benefits and assistance under emergency situations, etc. in reality, but this dissertation only focuses on the degree to which welfare state policies towards pension, long-term care and social assistance hypothetically cause poverty among older people if they do not have additional resources. Therefore, the definition of poverty is a theoretical concept referred to as "poverty risk for older people". Besides, low incomes in comparison with other residents in different countries do not show strict signs of the low living standard.

In the empirical part, I introduce the findings of a cross-national comparative study on the generosity conditions of ageing policy in Germany, Denmark, and the UK, regarding the hypothetical impact of different types of ageing policies on poverty of senior citizens in different types of welfare states. It shows that different welfare state's ageing policy differs in the degree and ways in which they frame poverty risk for older people. The welfare states of the three countries of the study represent different types of welfare regime according to the famous classification of Esping-Anderson (1990): the German welfare state which represents the conservative type of welfare regime, the Danish welfare state which represents the social democratic welfare regime, and the UK which represents the liberal type of welfare regime.

The third part of this dissertation provides an overview of the scientific literature about the concept of poverty, the role of welfare state policies for social inequality and poverty on old age and the role of welfare state policies in old age. In the fourth part, the dissertation introduces the theoretical concept of “ageing policy” and a theoretical typology of ageing policies. The fifth part introduces the methodological approach to the empirical study; it explains the measurement of poverty risk, the cross-national comparative approach and the selection of countries, the main dimensions of the comparative policy analysis for the single policy fields and the measurement of ageing policy as interaction of policy fields. The measurement of ageing policy is based on a new approach which measures the hypothetical impact of the interaction of three different policy fields in the context of ageing policies on poverty. In the sixth part, the dissertation analyses the differences in terms of generosity in the three different welfare state's ageing policies, and how they differ in their hypothetical impact on poverty of senior citizens. Part seven provides the conclusion and research approach in the future.

The dissertation makes an innovative contribution to the international scientific theorizing and research in the field, in which it offers a new, complex approach to the analysis of the impact of welfare state policies on poverty among older people. It also offers a new methodological approach for the measurement of the impact and findings from an empirical study to which applies the theoretical approach.

The main focus of the dissertation is restricted to three types of policies, pension policy and polities towards long-term care and social assistance. In addition, health policy and housing policy may also affect the poverty risk of older people. However, since this dissertation introduces a complex explanatory framework and a new method for its analysis, these two types of policies are not included.

Chapter 2　Literature Review

The European population is ageing. An increasing proportion of older people in the population belong to the clearest demographic characteristic of contemporary society (Zilova et al., 2014). Poverty among older people has long been an international issue which is widespread in many European countries (Adena and Myck, 2013). An older person is defined here as someone who is aged 65 or over, mainly because this is the most common statutory retirement age observed across many EU countries (Zaidi, 2010).

2.1　The concept of poverty

It has been mentioned that the definition of poverty in this dissertation follows the European Union's definition and thresholds recommended by the Statistic Office of the EU (Eurostat). But this dissertation only focuses on the degree to which welfare state policies towards pension, long-term care and social assistance hypothetically cause poverty risk among older people if they do not have additional resources. Therefore, the definition of poverty is a theoretical concept referred to as "poverty risk for older people". Of course, there has long been debated on what is poverty, poverty risk and poverty risk for older people in literature. Academic researches measure and explain poverty in different ways.

Spicker concludes that poverty is a hard-defined social phenomenon especially when it reaches a global scale (Spicker et al., 2007). "In European context poverty is often an elusive concept that is complicated to assess," (European Commission 2015, p. 140-141). The essential but difficult part to measure poverty is not just about finding suitable methods and criteria, it should also answer the question of what poverty exactly is, such as whether poverty should be measured as relative, or absolute one or see poverty as a consequence of income inequality, or as material deprivation (Brady, 2005; Kangas and Ritakallio, 2008). However, as authors have expressed:

If restricting the discussion to income poverty, absolute income poverty, put simply, asserts that there is some kind of (universal) income threshold under which the sustainment of human life and physical functional capacity becomes impossible, such as the UN definition "two dollars a day", whereas the relative definition uses the conception of "normal" living, and the possible exclusion from it, as its starting point (Nygård et al., 2017, p. 3).

The European Anti-Poverty Network (EAPN, 2009) has identified two different types of poverty as "absolute poverty" and "relative poverty". In 2006, another dimension was developed to measure poverty in the EU as material deprivation by the European Union Survey of Income and Living Conditions (EU-SILC). The definition was soon changed again. Five "Europe 2020" headline targets were agreed at the European Council meeting on 17th June 2010, including: "promoting social inclusion, in particular through the reduction of poverty, by aiming to lift at least 20 million people out of the risk of poverty and exclusion". An essential point expanded on the definition of social exclusion and poverty is "the population is defined as the number of persons who are at risk-of-poverty and exclusion according to three indicators (at-risk-of poverty; material deprivation; jobless household), leaving EU member states free to set their national targets on the basis of the most appropriate indicators, taking into account their national circumstances and priorities (European Council, 2010)." Additionally, another two different approaches were developed by two agencies to measure poverty. A Minimum Income Standards (MIS) approach which was developed by the Joseph Rowntree Foundation (JRF) and a Minimum Essential Budgets (MEB) approach which was employed by the Vincentian Partnership for Social Justice.

An absolute poverty standard is defined on purchase power which is sufficient to purchase the basic staff at the necessary point in time (Jäntti and Danziger, 2000; Dzkstra et al., 2014). Absolute poverty exists when people do not have the necessities for survival. This type of poverty is most common in developing countries. But groups of people such as homeless people in the EU (homelessness is persistent in most EU countries) still experience this type of extreme poverty (EAPN, 2009). The at-risk-of-absolute-poverty line made its first appearance in the world development report for poverty anticipation in 1990. The measures to create this "international poverty line" depend on two steps: "first, poverty lines for developing and low-income countries are collected and converted to international dollars using the latest Purchasing Power Parities (PPP) estimates. In the second step, the relationship between average consumption in a country (derived from national accounts) and the level of the poverty line is estimated" (Dotter, 2017, p. 3-4).

As new data has become available over the last twenty years, this poverty line has been updated many times, although the basic methodology has remained the same (Chen and Ravallion, 2000; Ravallion and Chen, 1996; Ravallion et al., 2009, 1991). Ravallion, Datt and van de Walle (1991) collected poverty lines for 33 countries from official and academic sources. They created a global poverty line of $1.01 per day at 1985 PPP prices by utilizing the poverty line shared by six countries including Tanzania, Morocco, Bangladesh, Indonesia, Nepal and Kenya. With new PPP estimates available, Chen and Ravallion (2001) updated this line. They utilized a middle line of $1.08 per day in the original database of the poorest ten countries. In 2009, with new PPP estimates available (ICP 2005), Ravallion, Chen and Sangraula integrated the previous poverty into international dollars. Following this, the World Bank provided another poverty estimate which was based on the 2011 PPP. This time the updated "international poverty line" was defined as $1.90 by updating the average of the 15 poorest nations' poverty lines (Ferreira et al., 2015).

A relative poverty standard, however, is defined in differently. According to the European Commission Joint Report on Social Inclusion:

"*people are said to be living in poverty if their income and resources are so inadequate as to preclude them from having a standard of living considered acceptable in the society in which they live. Because of their poverty they may experience multiple disadvantages through unemployment, low income, poor housing, inadequate health care and barriers to lifelong learning, culture, sport and recreation. They are often excluded and marginalized from participating in activities (economic, social and cultural) that are the norm for other people and their access to fundamental rights may be restricted* (*EAPN*, 2009, *p*. 5)."

In addition, the EAPN (2009) recommended a "multi-dimensional approach" to measuring material deprivation which is reflected in the "EU-SILC approach" in 2003. According to Zaidi (2010b: 14): "this indicator offers an absolute approach to reflect on incapacity to afford some items which are considered desirable or even necessary by most people to have adequate living standards".

Relative poverty measures have been used increasingly to describe the existence and development of poverty in Europe among academics and policy makers (Hoff, 2008). EU member states have agreed on using poverty indicators such as monetary indicators (Eurostat, 2005a). The relative poverty approach has been accepted and commonly used to measure poverty because it has many advantages. In the first place, relative poverty means that the at-risk-of-poverty threshold changes along with the economic development in the society. When the income value or social-economic situation changes, such as during an economic crisis or recession, the poverty threshold can drop instead of always being raised. Therefore, under this circumstance, the increase of the at-risk-of-poverty threshold for older people means that the income of the working population was raised at a much higher pace than the rising income for older people. In addition, as declared by the Directorate-General for Employment, Social Affairs and Inclusion of the European Commission and the Social Protection Committee: "... the relative character of the indicator which allows for international comparisons implies that it focuses more on poverty as social and economic exclusion than on poverty as a state of not having a given standard of living" (Directorate-General for Employment, Social Affairs and Inclusion of the European Commission and the Social Protection Committee, 2012).

As Smeeding reminds us "the purchasing power of a relative poverty standard will change over time as society-wide income or consumption change, while an absolute poverty standard will change only with the prices of commodities it can buy with currency exchange mechanisms to convert one currency's buying power into another" (Smeeding, 2015, p. 27). The relative poverty definition is widely used in most cross-international comparisons of poverty (Jäntti and Danziger, 2000; Dzkstra et al., 2014), especially in rich countries which rely heavily on an open and direct relative poverty definition. These tendencies reflect an important fact that an overall standard of living for older people can be indicated by the poverty standard and poverty threshold or by a minimum income standard (Brady and Burton, 2016).

In the European discussion especially in the comparative poverty research field, poverty is usually defined as an individual's inability to join in mainstream society due to the lack of adequate personal resources in which the most important resource is income. The debate on poverty risk in the population has long been discussed. In 2006, the EU published at-risk-of-poverty threshold was set to 60 percent of the national equalized median income in the total population (European Commission, 2006). And the at-risk-of-poverty rate for people aged 65+ measures the percentage of the population aged 65+ with income after social transfers below the at-risk-of-poverty threshold (European Commission, 2006). The indicator treats poverty as a comparative concept. This comparative element was explained in a broader sense which connects poverty with social inequality. But it still specifically focuses on the lower part of income distribution. However, among EU discussions, analyzing only the relative income statistics often failed to catch the important differences of living standards among the EU member states. As EU member states have been gradually enlarged, these differences have become increasingly apparent (Nelson, 2012). "It is true that the fruitfulness of non-monetary poverty indicators was recognized in the leading scholarly work related to the process of developing common benchmarks to evaluate social development in the EU countries" (Nelson, 2012, p. 149-150). Nevertheless, the EU has already monitored material deprivation in the process of social inclusion. This measure can complement the income-oriented definition of poverty well which was created earlier (Nelson, 2012).

As Blank (2008, p. 387) reminds us, "poverty is an inherently vague concept and developing a poverty measure involves some relatively arbitrary assumptions". In the long run, social scientists have shown much more interest in explaining poverty itself than in poverty measurements. However, it is a common belief that poverty data are essential indicators for basic needs.

Social science and sociologists usually use power, social structure, culture and the role of other factors that are commonly out of individuals' control to explain poverty. This school of thought is contrary to many economists' perspective that an individual can control their own fate, destiny and the way they reach their destinies under the "choice model". Therefore, an individual can control the cause of their own poverty (Piachaud, 1987). Some sociologists have even argued that poverty is functional in capitalist societies and is useful in a certain way (e.g. Gans, 1972). But another way to describe a similar term is "social exclusion". (Room, 1999; Hills, 1999; Glennerster et al., 1999).

Concepts of poverty and poverty measurements vary, and

poverty conceptual understandings have already existed all over the world for a longer time. As Smeeding states:

The conceptual underpinnings of poverty measures are anchored in economics (Lampman, 1964), sociology (Grusky and Kanbur, 2006), social statistics (Orshansky, 1965), and social policy (Rowntree, 1901; Booth, 1903). Income or living standards poverty measurement began in the Anglo-Saxon countries and dates back to at least to Rowntree (1901), who was the first to employ the concept of a poverty line in his empirical work on York, England, and that of Booth (1903) who invented the idea of a poverty line for London, the field has a meaningful social indicator of basic needs (Townsend, 1979, 1993; Piachaud, 1987; Ringen, 1985; Ravallion, 2014a). The United States (DeNavas-Walt et al., 2012) and the United Kingdom (Department for Work and Pensions, 2012) have long-standing "official" poverty series. In northern Europe and Scandinavia, the debate centers instead on the level of income at which minimum benefits for social programs should be set. In other words, their concept of insufficient "low income" is directly fed into programmatic responses to social needs (Bjöklund and Freeman, 1997; Marx and Nelson, 2013; Ravallion, 2014a; Smeeding, 2016, p. 23).

Nowadays, it is easy to find different poverty measurements. The World Bank uses harmonized measures that sometimes include micro data and secondary data. These data are based on income and consumption measures to reflect the living standard which is below a particular amount of income for each person for one day (Ravallion and Chen, 2011; Chen and Ravallion, 2012). Much of this work is centered on an absolute poverty threshold of $1.25 per person per day (Chen and Ravallion,

2010,2013;Ferriera and Ravallion,2009). In principle,poverty is a multidimensional concept and reflects many aspects of people's well being. In 1995,Europe adopted the official set of social indicators which includes explicit item of reducing poverty and social exclusion and the at-risk-of poverty indicator (Marlier et al.,2007).

Indeed, measurements of poverty strongly differ across countries,as Dotter and Klasen (2014,p.2) states:"While absolute poverty lines are typical for poverty measurement in developing countries, relative poverty is popular in developed countries. Relative income poverty lines are prevalent across Europe and the concept of relative poverty is generally accepted as more appropriate for advanced economies." These strongly accepted relative thresholds are often set at a fixed proportion,such as 40 percent to 60 percent of the mean or median income. These thresholds often account for social inclusion (Ravallion and Chen,2011).In addition,there has been a reemergence of deprivation measures and multidimensional poverty measurement in recent years. One of the most well-known cases is the UNDP's global multidimensional poverty index (MPI) for developing countries. The MPI is an index of "acute multidimensional poverty and reflects deprivations in core human functioning and rudimentary services (Alkire and Santos,2011,p.7)". The MPI includes three dimensions as Health, Education and Living standards with different aspects of indicators. The major contribution of MPI is a wide convergence of many different countries and it can be used in international comparison. Its supplementary index is "global happiness index" which further compensate an emotional dimension to capture additional functions and take moral indicator into consideration (UNDP,2014). Dotter (2014) has analyzed this

MPI measures and explains that this kind of measurement has already been used as an absolute concept that poverty cut-offs applied to do not various across time and space in many countries to measure different dimension of poverty in cross-national comparison research. In addition, many multidimensional poverty approaches which are typically country cases and regional cases are developed by many scholars (such as Alkire, Apablaza and Jung, 2014; D'Ambrosio et al., 2011; Guio et al., 2009; Whelan et al., 2014); Germany (Busch and Peichl, 2010; Rippin, 2013); Afghanistan (Trani et al., 2013); Buthan (Alkire et al., 2014; Santos and Ura, 2008); and Colombia (Salazar et al., 2013). These multidimensional poverty thresholds are often much more generous and coexist in rich countries. Therefore, comparing poverty outcomes under these multidimensional poverty thresholds is almost impossible due to their different indicators and using different data bases albeit they have the same methodology.

There are other poverty measurements, such as the measurement of material deprivation which uses the EU-SILC approach to this aspect of poverty, Zaidi claimed that:

... if an individual has an "enforced" lack of at least three of the following nine items they are deemed to be materially deprived: ability to face unexpected expenses; ability to pay for one week annual holiday away from home; existence of arrears (mortgage or rent payments, utility bills, or hire purchase installments or other loan payments); capacity to have a meal with meat, chicken or fish every second day; capacity to keep home adequately warm; and possession of a washing machine, a color TV, a telephone or a personal car (Zaidi, 2010b, p. 14).

However, from the late 1980s, multidimensional character of poverty has been accepted by many researchers. The French social policy discourse introduced a much broader definition of social exclusion also in the 1980s. But social exclusion is a much more comprehensive definition compared with poverty when referring mainly to a shortage of material resources (or income). Sen (1981) analyzed an inverse relationship between another material resource as "family power" with poverty. He states that family power stays in the place for help and ready for help even though food is available and there is no lack of income. He argues that this supportive force goes with a kind of basic disadvantage to handle poverty because the family power tends to transfer the assets into food or other necessary living materials by family members themselves but not by the market itself. And he believes that it is very important that market can transfer assets into food, which can be an essential way to decrease poverty in the social wide. However, Swift (1989) argues that the market cannot be solely responsible. Instead, the state must also provide possibilities to transfer assets into the basic necessities.

While anthropological approaches to poverty have often recognized its multidimensional nature, more traditional social science approaches poverty in terms of minimum subsistence needs, "... and then link these minimum needs to a minimum resource base to provide a measure of absolute poverty" (Yate, 2004, p. 26). What poor people have rather than what they do not have assumes that "the poor" are not helpless victims but owners and "strategy managers of complex asset portfolios" (Moser, 1998, p. 5; Narayan, 2000). This issue of agency is another important aspect of poverty. Often it has been anthropologists' work that has reminded us that "poor people" are not simply passive victims but have also developed coping strategies, various ways of managing their lives and dealing with impoverishment (Bridger and Pine, 1998; Caldwell, 2004; Glick Schiller, 2001).

The multidimensional approach of poverty is essential due to its evolvement from many social aspects that include various social characters. It is impossible that poverty and social welfare benefits are always presented in income assets or wealth (Chakravarty, 2009; Duclos and Araar, 2006; Haughton and Khandker, 2009; Wagle, 2008; Alkire et al., 2015). Many international research centers and institutions have created database and offered measures which are strictly based on the degree of each country's development for multidimensional poverty and deprivation (Villar, 2017). One of the famous multidimensional measurements is the European Union definition of "people at-risk-of-poverty", the others, for example, the "United Nations' Multidimensional Poverty Index".

Since the European Union employed the Europe 2020 poverty and social exclusion target (the European Union News, the European Commission, 2016), more attention is gradually being focused on multidimensional approaches to measure social exclusion and poverty (Kakwani and Silber, 2007). In justifying this approach, the EU Commission (2011) has indicated that "the computation of a single indicator is an effective way of communicating in a political environment, and a necessary tool in order to monitor 27 different national situations (p. 20)". However, progress towards this target is disappointing, which led to the failure to reduce poverty in 2015.

Other analysis reveals that "the union and intersection approaches to which European countries' multidimensional poverty measurement approach" which were developed by Alkire and Foster (2011) produce sharply contrasting results (Whelan et al.,2014). The result demonstrates that the multidimensional poverty measurement approach in European countries identifies quite small numbers comparing with multidimensional poverty in "better-off" nations.

In addition, the original headcount measurement was the most common method to monitor poverty. This measurement evaluates the poverty threshold in countries by including and calculating the actual number of poor people in the country (Basu and Stiglitz, 2016). However, as emphasized by Sen (1976, p. 219), "an unchanged number of people below the 'poverty life' may go with a sharp rise in the extent of the short-fall of income from the poverty line". "Large changes in incomes of the poor are ignored when the incomes stay below the poverty line, while small changes near the line can disproportionately affect measured poverty." as explained by Castleman et. al. (2015, p.3). Sen contends that "any government which focusing solely on headcount measures faces a strong temptation to concentrate on the richest among the poor, since this is the way that the number of the poor … can be most easily reduced" (Sen, 1992, p.105). And Bourguignon and Fields (1990) demonstrated that using headcount measures can encourage policy makers to tend to concentrate more on those people with an income which is slightly below the poverty line than those much poorer groups, and ignore the poorest poor.

Alternative poverty measures have been developed such as taking the intensity of social poverty into account to cover this problem. However, these measures can be considered as difficult for the public to understand and hard for policymakers to explain to the public, so that they are often excluded from policy discussions

(Basu and Stiglitz, 2016).

When people explain poverty, the conceptualization of poverty is a main issue of policy relevance and sociological importance. European contemporary poverty analysis has been heavily sustained affected by the Townsend's "relative deprivation approach" and the "relative income measures of poverty" which have continued to play the dominant role on measuring poverty in Europe (Hick, 2014).

Studies have also indicated that poverty in the post socialist states is different from other regions in Europe and the rest of the world. Many factors are important to explain new forms of poverty in the post socialist states. In Eastern Europe, many families possess capital assets but lack cash, which makes them different from other impoverished people in the rest of Europe (Kaneff and Pine, 2011). The former socialist states usually provided non-material social security services, for example, free health services and social assistance housing services and free or partly free education (usually except kindergarten). Nowadays, these social security services could have their theoretical impact in improving people's poverty (Kaneff, 2009), and certain kinds of the asset which people have possessed in abundance previously have now decreased in their original value, such as language skills or computer skills or industrial skills. On the contrary, other kinds of assets have increased their values such as space technology or neuroscience technology (Kaneff and Pine, 2011).

These changes could have transferred people's former poverty situation into new circumstances. Moreover, the social network involvement also makes the poverty situations different in socialist states. Large amounts of services and support could be obtained from family, neighbors and friends (Firlit and Chlopecki, 1992;

Pawlik, 1992). And in the socialist states, all these involvements have been reinforced many times (Caldwell, 2004; Ledeneva, 1998; Pine, 2002). Therefore, many things could be done, and drawbacks could be improved by the support from social network, such as having informal care services, handling emergency medical conditions and paying bills, finding a job, caring for babies and finding temporary babysitters or obtaining loans for basic living (Clarke 2002).

However, in a European context, many analyses of poverty have been turned towards the multidimensional approach. A large number of applications for multidimensional poverty have appeared under this approach (e.g. Cornomaldi and Zoli, 2012; Whelan et al., 2014; Wagle, 2008). A number of researchers have developed debates as well as discussions towards multidimensional poverty measures (e. g. Alkire and Foster, 2011; Alkire and Santos, 2010; Ravallion, 2011; Ferreira and Lugo, 2013). Nonetheless, as Hick indicated that "the problems of income-centric analysis are that they are very substantially problems of conceptualization, and the conceptualization of poverty remains a neglected aspect of this multidimensional turn to date" (Hick, 2014, p. 2). Besides, many authors have argued that it is necessary to have multidimensional indexes as the basic level data to further analyse multidimensional poverty (Whelan et al., 2014).

2.2 Poverty situation of older people

The old age poverty risk has been widely seen in terms of relative poverty which defines that social groups to become the poor are those living under "less than 60 percent of median income" in many European countries although the definition of relative poverty varies considerably.

In 2013, about 18 percent of the total population aged 65+ in the EU were in social exclusion or at poverty risk. The comparably low levels of income inequality result in a relatively small share of older people at-risk-of-relative poverty in some member states and mostly in Eastern Europe. There is a lower risk of poverty for older people aged 65+ which appeared in 22/28-member states in Europe. Older people aged 65 to 74 tend to have a relatively lower poverty risk compare to older people aged 75+ and the rest of older people groups. Obviously, older people aged 75+ and 90+ face a greatly more difficult living situation and are exposed to a higher risk of poverty (Social Protection Committee and the European Commission, 2015).

In the majority of EU member states, older people is more likely to have income below the poverty threshold (Lelkes, Medgyesi and Tóth Gyorgy, 2009). In comparative welfare research, low level of poverty risk, social and income inequality are usually highly noticeable in the Nordic countries (Nygård et al., 2017). Actually, all these features stand out the key elements of the "Nordic welfare model" and are considered to be the Nordic social welfare marks (e.g. Nygård, 2013; Kautto, 2001). Besides, the relative poverty risk rate of senior citizens in Scandinavian welfare states has decreased sharply since the 1960s. This is due to an introduction of "modern pension schemes" (Fritzell and Ritakallio, 2010; Gustafsson et al., 2009; Gustafsson and Pedersen, 1996; Gustafsson and Uusitalo, 1990). In countries such as Finland and Sweden, older people's income poverty has been at a relatively low level for several decades compared to the rest of Europe and the world (Eurostat, 2014; Ahonen, 2011). However, the problem of old age income poverty in these two countries has never disappeared. Despite Switzerland ranking among the wealthiest in the world and having one of the highest life expectancies, poverty among its residents who are older than age 64 is not negligible. Approximately one in five retired Swiss citizens has a monthly household income below the poverty threshold. This financial situation also has institutional implications because it is a formal precondition for accessing several social benefits, and many people live just above the threshold thanks solely to such assistance. It is a common paradox in welfare regimes that a situation of vulnerability, when socially recognized, confers rights to receive support from public institutions (Oris et al., 2017).

Authors such as Zaidi (2010) claimed that Latvia has the highest rate of old age poverty risk for older people aged 65+. The author identified the average risk of the poverty condition for senior citizens in EU27 in the year 2008, and the UK came the fifth highest. This is a result which contrasts with Zaidi's (2006) figures in 2003. Then, in 2014, some 15 countries had a lower rate of poverty in the 65+ age group than the UK according to a renewed report by the International Longevity Centre (ILC-UK). Britain's pensioners are some of the worst off in the EU and are at a greater risk of falling into poverty (ILC-UK, 2014).

The main theoretical argument in the scientific literature for the explanation of poverty in older age has shown general impact factors on old age poverty. In a book published more than a century ago that remains influential, Rowntree (1901) analyzed the family cycle and identified poverty in old age as the norm for the western working class. Considerable research in social history and historical demography has also confirmed this assessment (Oris et al., 2015).

2.3 The role of welfare states policies for social inequality and poverty in the old age in the welfare state's theory

2.3.1 Theorizing the relationship between the welfare states policy, social inequality and poverty in the 1980s.

The welfare states aim to implement social policies to protect citizens. In the cases when older people stop working in need of long-term care or medical care due to declining body functions, the welfare states should offer support due to these difficulties. The main theoretical argument on the role of the welfare states' policy for poverty in old age has shown that the welfare state has a primary role in guaranteeing living standards and basic living rights.

The establishment of welfare states and universal pension schemes in most Western countries after the Second World War has contributed to a reduction of old age poverty in a later period. The proportion of poor people among the older people in the 1970s remained very high, a fact highlighted by the scholars who initiated the political economy of aging in those years (Minkler and Estes, 1990; Phillipson, 1981; Walker, 1981). The French sociologist Serge Paugam (1991) explained that an individual needed to contribute to the welfare system for a long period to obtain a full pension after their retirement.

However, the spending patterns and generosity level of social policy of welfare states differ depend on their policy structure and policy goals. Many scholars have analyzed various factors to explain different policy responses of welfare states. A main theoretical concept in comparative welfare state research that is important for the relationship between social policy and poverty is the concept of "de-commodification" which was proposed by Esping-Andersen (1990). He defines "de-commodification" to "the degree to which individuals, or families, can uphold a socially acceptable standard of living independently of market participation" in his distinguished work, The Three Worlds of Welfare Capitalism (Esping-Anderse, 1990, p. 37). On the basis of a high level of de-commodification, welfare states policy does not only guarantee the basic living condition and establish basic safety net for citizens, but they further de-commodify citizen's living condition in order to let them choose freely not to take market participation without worry about incomes. If a welfare state offers generous de-commodification, individuals have rights to pensions, sickness insurance, unemployment benefits that guarantee an income at the level of normal earnings.

2.3.2 The theoretical approach of Esping-Andersen

The empirical case study of this dissertation exams the ageing policy in German, Denmark and the UK according to the celebrated welfare state's classification approach by Esping-Andersen (1990). In his work, he also measures the relationship between welfare states policy, social inequality and poverty in general. He argues that how do welfare states protect citizens from social inequality and social poverty.

De-commodification happens if people in society can manage their life without relying on the market and get social services as rights. According to Esping-Andersen (1990), welfare states differ with their degree of de-commodification. In the social assistance welfare states model, this kind of right has actually strengthened the market because those people who have failed in the market have to "contract private-sector welfare" (Esping-Andersen, 1990, p. 22). In the compulsory social insurance welfare states, such as Germany, which was the forerunner of typical social insurance policy, social insurance benefits have depended on contribution and work performance. The degree which people are presented with social de-commodifying rights relates to the extent to which social program provides choices to market dependence.

To measure different degrees of inequality by variations in the de-commodifying potential of actual social policies, rules and standards are examined and crucial dimensions are measured. In his work, the first dimension manages individual's access to social benefits, in his words: "eligibility rules and restrictions on entitlements (Esping-Andersen, 1990, p. 47)". The second dimension governs people's income replacement. And the third dimension has to do with "the range of entitlement" (Esping-Andersen, 1990, p. 49). However, in the real world, there are no welfare states with only one dimension in any pure cases and every country has a rather mixed system. He then distinguishes the variability of welfare states' capability to de-commodification by showing the de-commodification scores for three social welfare policy fields which are "pension, sickness, and the unemployment cash benefits". All these scores draw the pictures of how easy and how hard an individual leave the market to get social benefit with different conditions. In the first place, scores describe the precondition for eligibility such as working life contribution and experiences. Secondly, they summarize the waiting period to access to benefit as well as duration period to be entitled to benefits.

Thirdly, they demonstrate variety of benefit degrees. As a result, the Nordic countries, in particular are "de-commodifying", the conservative countries are, as usual, in the middle, while the liberal countries are consistently to be the least. This result perfectly matches his expected welfare states regime typology.

Esping-Andersen defines the welfare states in his book as "a system of stratification":

"*The welfare state is not just a mechanism that intervenes in, and possibly corrects, the structure of inequality; it is, in its own rights, a system of stratification. It is an active force in the ordering of social relations* (*Esping-Andersen*, 1990, *p*. 23).

The welfare states can provide citizens with social security and social services and keep social order. But they have various capabilities concerning social equality in cross-national comparison. In the conservative countries such as Germany, the redistribution influences are rather minimized, while in Nordic countries such as Denmark, this effect is tremendous (Sawyer, 1982; Hewitt, 1977; Stephens, 1979; O'Higgins, 1985; Ringen, 1987; Ringen and Uusitalo, 1990). The reason why there is a big difference in distribution consequences is that social transfer in the welfare states as a major measure to deal with redistribution has replaced the tax systems. The larger the welfare states are, the heavier financial requirements they need. Therefore, the welfare states have to implement heavy taxes, as a result, the redistribution influence shift to mainly depend on social transfer.

Due to welfare states' different capability on structuring equality, they have different abilities to reduce and eliminate poverty especially for certain social groups, such as older people. In the famous "Luxembourg Income Study", it shows that there is

29 percent of older people in poverty range in the UK, while the figure is 11 percent in Germany but less than 1 percent in Sweden (Hedström and Ringen, 1987; Smeeding et al., 1988). As older people group highly relies on social income transfer and sickness payment, these figures present different welfare state's system has various impacts on social inequality and poverty.

2.3.3 Esping-Andersen's typology of welfare regimes and their roles for social inequality and poverty

In the world of welfare states, making classifications and describing their characteristics are the nonstop mission for welfare researchers. "The welfare states variations are not linearly distributed" is found by Esping-Andersen (Esping-Andersen, 1990, p. 26-27), who clusters the welfare states by "types of welfare regimes".

Among his three clusters, for the "liberal welfare states" it is a typical characteristic that the market is encouraged by the state to cater private welfare benefit scheme or guarantee the minimum welfare benefit. These countries effectively include social rights and build order of stratification. Typical example nations in this cluster are the United States and Canada.

In his second cluster, social insurance is the major characteristic. In contrast to the "liberal welfare states", they concern of gender matter more than the participation of the market. Non-working house wives are excluded from social insurance, and mother-hood is encouraged by family benefits. The main principle of this cluster is that family has the responsibility to serve their members until their ability and sources are exhausted when the state interferes. Women's poverty condition in this cluster is serious than men especially after their retirement or being widows. Older women have higher risk of facing social inequality and poverty. This type of welfare states includes countries such as Germany, France, Austria and Italy. However, the conservative European countries have more and more integrated into liberal and social democratic model, for example, Germany has become less corporative and more social democratic (Hemerijck, 2013).

In his third cluster of welfare states, de-commodification of social rights was extended. Social policy is to emancipate citizens from the market and the family. Their main principle is to maximize the ability of an individual and reduce the dependence on family, which is in contrast to the conservative welfare states regime. The social democratic welfare regime offers universal social rights related to social security and social services, at a high level of generosity. Social Democratic regimes will not wait until the traditional family capability is exhausted. But this type of welfare regimes has relatively heavy financial burden, therefore higher tax rate is required even for the middle-income class. As Esping-Andersen explains that "all benefit, all are dependent, and all will presumably feel obliged to pay" (Esping-Andersen, 1990).

2.3.4 The critical debate about Esping-Andersen' welfare state regime approach after 1990

The debates about concepts of welfare regime in comparative welfare research have never stopped. Criticism of Esping-Andersen's welfare state regime approach after 1990 mostly concentrates on whether country profiles are fit well the regime clusters or if certain countries should be classified in differently. Critical debates also focus on the gender issues and the missing of women roles in the welfare states typology. Many other welfare states researcher defined the welfare states in their own ways.

Concerning the classification of welfare states, one of the important criticisms of Esping-Andersen's typology is that he did not consider the Mediterranean countries characteristics which Italy belongs to, and countries like Greece, Portugal and Spain did not include in his typology. Another criticism is that the "Antipodean" countries' (Australian and New Zealand) are included in the "liberal welfare regime type". Many critics believe that these Antipodean countries do not fit in the "liberal regime type" because they have a higher degree of social protection than the liberal welfare regime type ideal type. Although their public welfare benefit highly relies on the means-tested model, yet these two countries' means-tested model is the most comprehensive system with income support benefits. Instead of social programs, redistribution effect has been carried out by "employment security" and "wage control". Therefore, it is argued that these countries ought to belong to an extra welfare state's cluster (Castles, 1998; Hill, 1995; Korpi and Palme, 1998).

Some authors have introduced other typologies for the classification of welfare states. Leibfried (1992) classified welfare states as "Anglo-Saxon/Residual model" (represented by United States, Australia, New Zealand and the UK), "Bismarck/Institutional model" (represented by Germany and Austria), "Scandinavian/Modern model" (represented by Sweden Norway Finland and Denmark) and "Latin Rim/Rudimentary model" (represented by Spain, Portugal, Greece, Italy and France) by poverty policy and social insurance dimensions. Castle and Mitchell (1993) introduced their welfare state types on the basis of dimensions like welfare expenditure and benefit equality as "Liberal type" (include Ireland, Japan, Switzerland and the United States), "Conservative type" (include West-Germany, Italy and Netherlands), "Non-right Hegemony type" (include Belgium, Denmark, Norway and Sweden) and "Radical type" (include Australia, New Zealand and the UK). Siaroff (1994) distinguishes welfare state types as "Protestant liberal" (involve Australia, Canada, New Zealand and the UK), "Advanced Christian-democratic" (involve Austria, Belgium, France and West-Germany), "Protestant social-democratic" (involve Denmark, Finland, Norway and Sweden), and "Late female mobilization" (involve Greece, Ireland, Italy and Japan) on the basis of three dimensions: family welfare orientation, female work desirability and extent of family benefits being paid to women. Korpi and Palme (1998) introduce a welfare state typology based on entitlement, benefits principles and governance of social insurance programs. Their typology includes "Basic security type" (Canada, Denmark, Netherlands, New Zealand, Switzerland, Ireland, the UK and United States), "Corporatist type" (Austria, Belgium, France, Germany, Italy and Japan), "Encompassing type" (Finland, Norway and Sweden), "Targeted type" (Australia), and "Voluntary state subsidized type". However, the welfare regime typology of Esping-Andersen is the most popular one in social sciences. One reason is that it is theoretically more complex than the other typologies, and that different to the other authors, Esping-Andersen has also introduced a theoretical approach that offers an explanation why the European welfare regimes are different, the "class coalition theory" (Esping-Andersen, 1990).

Other critical debates on Esping-Andersen's welfare regime

approach pointed out that his approach did not include a typology for developing countries (Mares and Carnes,2009). Other researchers proposed different welfare state type especially for "poor" countries, such as "insecure regime type" (Wood and Gough,2006). Wildeboer Schut and his colleagues proposed an "undefined" welfare states type based on the Esping-Andersen's typology (Wildeboer Schut et al.,2001).

Critics around Esping-Andersen's gender issue involves the missing gender effects in the concept of de-commodification (for example, Daly, 1994; Hobson, 1994; Lewis, 1992), the missing role of women in the analysis of welfare state, and the lacking family provision in the part of social benefit research (for example, Borchost, 1994; Bussemaker and Kersbergen, 1994; Daly,1994). Critics also revolve that the whole typology of the welfare states clusters relatively ignore the women's roles in the analysis (for example, Langan and Ostner, 1991; Lewis, 1992; Borchost, 1994; Bussemaker and Kersbergen, 1994; Daly, 1994; Hobson, 1994; Lewis and Ostner, 1995; Sainsbury, 1994, 1999). It was also criticised that the typology neglects the gender effects in the provision of social stratification and social rights. As a result, feminists came up with new and alternative typologies of welfare states which include gender effects albeit they usually have shown their limitations, such as some of them only include one factor (Sainsbury,1999), some only use a small number of profiled nations (Lewis,1992). Other researchers in the recent days such as Dowd (2013) criticizes Esping-Andersen's simplification of the three welfare regime models as un-regarding of both genders, and un-consideration about the unpaid labor contributed caring work by women. "Until the value of unpaid caring work done by women is included, welfare state typology will be incomplete"

(Dowd, 2013, p. 11). Dowd believed that women's roles are different concerning de-commodification and social stratification which can hardly be included as equality of citizen rights in the Esping-Andersen's research method.

Welfare state researchers have developed definitions of welfare state in their ways and the welfare state means different things in different countries. Some researchers criticize the concept of welfare state regimes by Esping-Andersen's approach. For example, Kasza (2002) has questioned that "the concept of welfare regimes is not a workable basis for research" (2002, p. 283). Others defined welfare state by analyzing separate welfare state clusters with corresponding characteristics, and the debate about welfare states has never stopped.

2.4 The role of welfare states policies in old age

2.4.1 Situation of people in older age and poverty risk

People in the old age have a different living situation compare with other social groups because most of them leave the labor market and face higher risk of decreased body functions. Around the year 2014, many surveys and researchers have found that the decreased shift of poverty risk among older people, and the lowest poverty rate appeared in 2014. One of the main reasons was that social policies which aimed to support this age group were successfully implemented. Older people aged 65 to 74 tends to have a relatively lower poverty risk compare to older people aged 75+. Older people aged 75+ and 90+ faces much more difficult living condition and are exposed to much higher poverty risk (Council of the European Union, 2016). However, albeit the relative upturn situation, nowadays, older people still face high risk of poverty and serious gender difference. Gender difference is greater in the older cohort such as 75+ and 85+ than the younger old age cohort. In the age group of the oldest old, large percent of women are widows who suffer higher risk of poverty (Federal Statistical Office, 2016). In the past 15 years, the decrease of the at-risk-of-poverty rate for older people happens mostly in the East European countries. Some conservative welfare states such as Germany have seen the increase in this figure. People in the Nordic countries have been experienced lowest the at-risk-of-poverty risk compare with other European countries. The relative poverty risk rate of senior citizens in the Nordic welfare states have decreased sharply since the 1960s. This is due to an introduction of the "modern pension schemes" (Nygård et al., 2017). In countries such as Finland, older people's income poverty has been at a relatively low level for several decades compared to the rest of Europe and the world (Eurostat, 2014; Ahonen, 2011) However, Sweden has increased poverty rate in the last decades.

2.4.2 International differences regarding people's living conditions in old age

Living conditions of older people describe a picture of the social situation which is related to income, poverty and social inequality, life satisfaction, and social protection conditions.

Older people are the high-risk population group of poverty, this is the situation in most of the European countries. Besides, gender difference exit along with social exclusion according to the report "Living Condition in Europe" by the Eurostat in 2014: women is the group who faces a greater risk of population and social exclusion than the whole population, while people aged 65 to 75 experienced lower poverty rate among the population in most of the EU member states, however, in Malta, Cyprus, Belgium, Slovenia, Croatia and Bulgaria, the at-risk-of-poverty rate for older people is much higher than the younger age groups.

2.4.3 The role of different fields of welfare state policy in old age

2.4.3.1 The role of welfare states in general for poverty in old age

Welfare states aim to reduce poverty and remedy the market mechanism holes which could cause the weakness in citizen life. Usually, welfare states provide social policies to protect their citizens at different degrees when they suffer being child, ageing, illness, injuries, unemployment and retirement. But the social policy pattern and generosity levels of welfare states are different according to their social structure, goals, financial capability and budget. Therefore, poverty reducing outcomes largely depend on coping strategies. Of course, welfare states have kept changing their social policies and capability to reduce poverty all these years. Aging is one of the most challenges issues that welfare states have to deal with in the process of reducing poverty. The aging population is the heavy burden of welfare program budget since they are making less contribution but need increasing benefits. Some social insurance-oriented welfare states such as Germany implemented pension insurance contributions after retirement to reduce this burden. However, this is still a serious problem especially when older people have health care and long-term care needs. Many welfare states have released this burden by relatively increasing tax rates for labor force and minimum years of contribution or entitlement age, and encourage older people to postpone retirement to increase contribution period by providing deferred retirement benefits or reemployment. Nevertheless, reemployment of older people is usually related to low quality and low pay jobs which could cause higher poverty risk (Lee and Koo, 2017).

However, many scholars have also questioned if the welfare states reduce poverty. We can easily review literature theoretically and empirically on this point. Murray and Mead have then questioned the effectiveness of welfare states' social program towards poverty, and comprehensive welfare programs reduce working incentives. They have questioned that welfare state did not achieve what they aimed to do (Murray, 1984; Mead, 1997).

Sommers and Block presented "perversity thesis" which analyzes that the welfares states have made poor people's poverty condition worse by encouraging them to rely on the social welfare benefits instead of actively rejoining the market, and this tendency has a descendible characteristic (Sommers and Block, 2005). The relationship between welfare states and poverty is a contradictory condition was presented in the literature by scholars such as Korpi, Palme, Brady and Burroway. They believe that "social policies with low ceilings for earnings replacement, targeted programs and basic security programs stimulate program exit among the middle classes and increase the demand for private insurance" (Korpi and Palme, 1998, p. 682). And parts of social policies do reduce poverty while other parts are unclear or lack of evidence to proof (Brady and Burroway, 2012).

2.4.3.2 The role of pension systems for poverty in old age

Some authors argue that pension policies are particularly relevant for older people's poverty risk. In most European countries, the public pension system and other pension fields play their roles in protecting older people from poverty risks. Pension schemes ensure that they retain the same living standards as the rest of the population and continue to support older people to handle care costs. An important feature of old age poverty explained by Carlos Farinha Rodrigues and Isabel Andrade in their articles is income distribution. There is a difference between the average relatively young older people group's income and the much older group's income. The former has a higher average income. More than 16 percent of older people are involved in income distribution (Rodrigues and Andrade, 2013). With the contributive pension and means-tested pension scheme evolution, older people poverty was reduced and older people's standards of living have been improved to some extent. However, this evolution might have been reversed by the European austerity policies which were implemented after 2010 which has had a strong impact on pension policy schemes (Rodrigues and Andrade, 2013). Pension benefit is the main income source of older people, old age poverty largely depends on welfare state's public-private pension design (Ebbinghaus, 2016). With the absence of public pension schemes, almost all European countries would be faced with a significantly higher poverty risk for older people. For example, France would have the highest old-age poverty risk at more than 90 percent. This part of the figure is attained by 12.4 percent public GDP spending. Italy and Austria have similar situations. The public pension programs are very important in countries like the Czech

Republic and the Netherlands, the old age poverty condition would be extremely high without this pension scheme (Kidd, 2009).

Additionally, retirement schemes for individuals have an important impact in countries such as Portugal, Belgium, Spain, the United Kingdom and Greece. More and more, these countries have an additional means-tested old age income program. This pension scheme offers a certain pension payment when individuals or the family fall into a designated level. However, these payments do not prevent people from living in poverty risk (Haitz, 2015). Studies show that old age poverty does not affect all pensioner groups equally, older pensioners are more likely to be vulnerable, have higher expenditure needs and/or face discrimination in Europe (Carrera et al., 2011).

Analyzing poverty rates across Europe reveals considerable variation. The Nordic and Dutch basic pension systems, which have been marked as relatively generous programs in welfare states, are found to have the lowest poverty rates. In contrast, the UK and Ireland which have lean Bismarck types with basic social security system are found to have the highest poverty rates. In other countries, contributory public or private pensions lead to significant levels of inequality above the at-risk-of-poverty line (Ebbinghaus, 2016). The Social Protection Committee and the Directorate General for Employment, Social Affairs and Inclusion of the European Commission concluded that older people poverty risk is higher than poverty risk of population aged 0～64 in 2014. Older people's social exclusion risk under pension incomes index is also higher than the other group (SPC, 2016). Other authors argue that generosity level of pension benefit has been decreased significantly because of pension reforms, and measurements connected to pension contributions and pension benefits have resulted in pension systems becoming less progressive. This has led to concerns that these systems are inadequate for older people (Grech, 2014).

Many countries have found a significant negative correlation between the generosity of public pension and poverty risk such as Estonia, Australia, Italy and Malta. However, in Cyprus and Ireland, the at-risk-of-poverty rate decreased because of their much more generous pension system. Nevertheless, the decline in the levels of generosity for pension by pension reforms can lead to the increase of the at-risk-of-poverty rate for older people aged 65+ (Zaidi et al., 2006). Analysis have concluded that these reforms may result in a decrease of pension payments level. For many countries, the minimum pension can be lower than domestic poverty threshold (Schähl, 2007: 330; Riedmüller and Willert, 2007).

However, in countries such as Norway, Denmark and Switzerland, older people poverty risk is lower due to the provision of some kind of basic pension with "a uniform amount". The protection afforded by these safety nets is mostly based on residence identity or citizenship in these countries, although these kinds of benefit are independent of earnings (Haitz, 2015). The effectiveness of the minimum pension further helps reduce poverty in some European welfare states such as Denmark, which is due to the already near-comprehensive nature of the basic pension schemes (Mantovani et al., 2005).

Taxation reforms in many countries have changed retirement benefits. For example, the Retirement Income Act ("Alterseinkünftegesetz") implemented in 2005 in Germany has reduced pension payments when they are paid out in old age. This reduced part of the pension payment has been treated as a form of old age income compared with the pre-reform condition when old age pension payments were tax-free besides revenue share. Another example which indicates that taxation reforms have changed retirement benefits is in the UK. Until now, older people must pay tax when their total annual income is more than their Personal Allowance (up to 11,000 pounds/12,540 euros) in the UK according to the UK government regulations, which means that if older people's annual income is higher than 11,000 pounds they need to pay tax at a rate which varies from 20% to 45% (UK government statistics, 2017). Nevertheless, the first 25% of the amount built up in any pension is still allowed as a tax-free lump sum. Usually, a pensioner's basic income is lower than the UK's tax thresholds, i.e., the full new state pension in the UK is currently 750 euros per month (164.35 pounds per week) (UK government statistic, 2017).

Therefore, it is important that older people can access stable, long-term and reliable income sources. According to the report from the International Labor Organization's World Social Protection Report from 2014 to 2015, when population approach to old age, the majority is unable to assess to high-paid or well-paid jobs. But this situation could be different when older people have personal savings and private assets. However, it is hard to anticipate whether these personal savings and private assets are sufficient to assure older people have an appropriate quality of life. Besides, although family transfer can be another additional source to protect older people, this source is unstable, especially for those family members who are already living in poverty or suffering from health problems. European older people income security also relies more on other publicly free or low-rate social benefits such as long-term care benefits and social assistance benefits. The highly educated or professional older people could continue to possess reliable payments from occupation until the very late of their lives, but these people represent only a small portion of older people population. Therefore, older people will be pushed to face poverty risk if welfare states' social benefits are not accessible (International Labor Organization, World Social Protection Report 2014/15).

Overall, older people's main income source is pension, together with social benefits programs such as long-term care and social assistance which contribute to a whole picture of old age security. A low level of pension income, insufficient social assistance benefit, or high charges for long-term care services cannot guarantee protection against poverty for older people because they are unable to provide adequate support for these people (Heinrich, 2000).

2.4.3.3 The role of long-term care policies for poverty in old age

Other authors argue over the role of long-term care policies with regard to its impact on old age poverty risk. Informal and formal care resources stay at the balance for long-term care policies. When informal care is unreachable or invariable, formal care must back up, otherwise, poverty will appear. Therefore, economic poverty increases the poverty risk when formal care programs are unable to identify an individual's care needs and informal care schemes cannot back up in time (Kröger, 2009). Similarly, when older people lack both formal and informal care, they face poverty (Chou & Kröger, 2014).

Moreover, Kröger and Leinonen argued that, with regard to care for older people, there is the social right to access to public care services. However, access is somehow restricted to those with the greatest care needs, therefore public services only partially cover existing needs (Kröger and Leinonen, 2012). This has brought an increasing need to supplement the gaps in public provision either by purchasing private services or by extending the amount of family care (Meagher and Szebehely, 2013), therefore exposing these potential care recipients with poverty risk. But in the Nordic welfare state model, public responsibility and universalism are the main principles; long-term care benefits cover the whole population (Puthenparambil et al., 2017).

According to the report Adequate social protection for long-term care needs in an ageing society by the Social Protection Committee and the European Commission, more European older people are expected to experience long-term care needs. These groups of older people require care and medical services on an increasing basis. On average, older people in Europe usually live for no more than 15 years without experiencing health issues which limit their ability to control and handle their normal living activities. Long-term care needs increase substantially for people aged 80 and over (Social Protection Committee and the European Commission, 2014).

In almost all European member states, family care givers and informal care services have played an important role in supporting older people with long-term care needs. In many states, families are responsible for providing long-term care services as well as financial care support for their old family members, while other states strengthen this legal informal care responsibility and ensure care needs are met by monitoring care services. However, there is no similar legal framework of offering long-term care services in the EU, and there are various degrees of accessible and available formal and informal long-term care services and benefits across the EU [Social Protection Committee

(SPC) and the European Commission (DG EMPL),2015].

It has been found that poverty matters for health outcomes in later life in 12 European countries, including the Czech Republic and Poland. Wealth-defined and subjective poverty correlates much more strongly with health outcomes than income-defined measure (Adena and Myck, 2013). As people become older and after retirement, the risk of falling into poverty increases steeply. Older people often have lower work ability with the reduction of their income, and they experience worse health conditions than the other age groups of population, which can lead to a higher degree of economic expenditure. Some parts of older people face disability consequences. All of these problems can lead to older people falling into a serious poverty risk (Kidd, 2009).

Compared with the literature on pension policy and poverty in old age, studies of the long-term care policy field and poverty in old age are relatively sparse. The recent 3-year OECD Health Project found that "pensioners are frequently required to contribute to funding long-term care, both by directly contributing to the public system and in the form of substantial private cost-sharing" (OECD, 2015, p.14). Other studies found that long-term care and poverty conditions impact on each other under laws and regulations which are designed to pay long-term care contributions (James, 2014). However, long-term care financing policy could help to reconcile access to care. Most governments provide older people with financial support programs for long-term care costs or personal help services. For example, Germany set up a strong social insurance system which includes long-term care insurance. Denmark has set up a comprehensive and universal social care system which includes a tax refund scheme. Belgium covers most of its older people's long-term care cost with the health care system. For countries which do not have a particularly long-term care coverage system, most of them have universal personal care benefits schemes, such as Austria, Italy and France (in the form of in cash), and such as New Zealand or Australia (in the form of in-kind) (OECD, 2011).

The German "long-term care insurance act" was introduced in 1995 and 1996, and long-term care responsibility for older people was defined as a task for the state. "But older people only have the right to receive paid care if they can prove that they have a physical need for it through illness and disability", according to the act (§ 14 Abs. 1 SGB Ⅺ). In 2015, this law was amended again and care benefit was raised. However, there is problems concerning care provision for people with dementia and 24-hour care who live at home (Doehner and Rothgang, 2006; Theobald and Hampel, 2013). In Germany, up to the mid-1990s, the family mainly provided elderly care, which was unpaid and not defined as "work" (Pfau-Effinger et al., 2009). Now, however, the care allowance benefits provide payment, albeit at a low level, to family members who provide care services for certain a length of time. The payment is paid directly to care recipients but not to the care giver. Among older people who receive care allowance according to the "long-term care insurance", 69.3 percent of them live in their own households. In this group, the percentage of those who were cared for exclusively by family care givers was 67 percent in 2009 (Eichler & Pfau-Effinger, 2009; Motel-Klingebiel, 2002, 2004; Statistisches Bundesamt, 2009). In 2017, a second bill to strengthen German long-term care was passed and implemented. Long-term care need assessment standards were modified from three levels to five care grades, which dropped the precondition that people must prove they have physical needs for long-term care through illness and disability, and dementia cases are all integrated into care grades benefits. Furthermore, after the introduction of German social insurance which was based on long-term care insurance, many families' financial pressure to care of their old family members has been eased.

There are steep increases in the need for care among some age groups. In Germany, the need for long-term care rises sharply beyond certain ages, from 75～79, when one in every ten persons needs care, while in the 80～85 age group, the figure is approximately one in every five. In the 90+ age group, the proportion increases to approximately two thirds, with 50 percent being cared for in a care home. The German aging population requires more care and women are more dependent on long-term care than men (Federal Statistical Office, Older people in Germany and the EU, 2016).

According to figures from EU-SILC, 93 percent of older people aged 65 and over received health care in EU 28 while there are also parts of older people who are in a frail situation with low income in other member states facing difficulties to receiving health care. EU-SILC reports in 2003 showed three main reasons why older people have unsatisfied care needs: "too expensive" "too far to travel" or "long waiting lists" (EU-SILC, 2003). In general, older people with low income have much higher unmet care needs than those with higher income. In the same year, the lowest degree of unmet care needs was found in Denmark, Austria and Slovenia, while the highest degree of unmet care needs was found in Greece, Romania and Latvia [Social Protection Committee (SPC) and the European Commission (DG EMPL), 2015].

2.4.3.4 The role of policies towards social assistance for poverty in old age

It is also argued that social assistance policy has a great impact on old age poverty, but relevant literature is less substantial. Several authors support the view that social welfare programs reduce poverty to a certain degree. For example, Kenworth examined social assistance policy field by evaluating the impacts of social welfare policy's extensiveness on poverty rates. The research referred to 15 industrialized nations from 1960 to 1991 and the results strongly support the idea that social benefit programs reduce poverty:

… social-welfare policies do help to reduce poverty, even when indirect, dynamic effects are taken into account. The unstandardized coefficient in the equation with government transfers used as the social-welfare policy measure indicates that, on average for these 15 *nations, each additional* 1% *of GDP spent on transfers over the period* 1960-91 *may have reduced the absolute poverty rate in the early* 1990*s by as much as* 75 *percentage points* (*Kenworth*, 1999, *p*. 13).

Studies of other authors refer to the social assistance policy in Sweden. This policy provides a safety net for older people and families facing financial hardship, as in most welfare states.

Böckman argues that "for the major part of the 20th century, levels of social assistance receipt were largely characterized by stability, and fluctuation simply followed variations in unemployment rates and the business cycle in Sweden" (Böckman, 2011, p. 486).

Social assistance is often a crucial instrument in addressing all forms of poverty in the European welfare state. An abundant cash transfer can help protect older people from poverty risk immediately, although this kind of assistance benefit level is often, in practice, lower than the recipient's needs. More importantly, cash transfers in social assistance schemes could have a much larger impact on decreasing poverty (International Labor Organization and World Social Protection Report, 2014/15). For example, Woolard, Harttgen and Klasen have argued that poverty risk in South Africa has been reduced by its non-contributory grants (Woolard et al., 2010). Skoufias and Parker concluded that "the Opportunities Programme" in Mexico helps to reduced poverty by 10 percent (Skoufias and Parker, 2001), and the World Bank claimed that "Kyrgyzstan's Social Protection Programme" reduced the 24 percent of "extreme poverty" while reducing poverty gap by 42 percent (World Bank, 2003).

However, cash transfers have the drawback of being only a short-term solution which cannot reduce older people poverty risk in the long run. It is crucial that social assistance policy scheme should enable to bring older people out of poverty risk for good because "the risk of falling back into poverty is extremely high where effective social protection mechanisms do not exist" (Chronic Poverty Advisory Network, 2014, p. 3).

Other social assistance programs available in different countries mainly refer to housing support, such as a program of "providing social assistance through implementing a differentiated approach" in Bulgaria. This is about some targeted social allowances which provide grants to rent municipal houses. This allowance is intended to reduce old age poverty and is targeted at those aged 70+ and who live alone. The exact amount of payment depends on the rent. In addition, a monthly allowance is also paid to satisfy incidental health and any other essential care needs for older people. The System of Assistance in Material Need (SAMN) is another social assistance scheme available in the Czech Republic to support individuals and families on housing costs if these costs more than 30 percent of their total income.

In Luxembourg, a means-tested general social assistance "Revenue Minimum Garanti-RMG" is available also for older people. To receive benefits, pension entitlements must be below the RMG-threshold. In 2015, the RMG minimum benefits were 1,348 for single households, 2,022 for households with two adults and around 386 for each additional adult in the same household [Social Protection Committee (SPC) and the European Commission (DG EMPL), 2015].

In addition, Nelson analyzed the link between social assistance benefit levels and material deprivation in Europe:

> *It is shown that the relationship between assistance and deprivation is negative, indicating that material deprivation is less extensive in countries with higher benefit levels. The influence of other relevant contextual effects does not change this relationship to any serious extent. There was no clear effect of public services or active labor market policy on material deprivation, factors essential in the EU discussion on poverty and social inclusion. The results demonstrate that the role of social assistance in combating material hardships should perhaps be strengthened in future EU policy frameworks* (*Nelson*, 2012, *p*. 148).

Means-tested benefits are usually the direct form of social assistance systems. Social assistance policies reallocate income and social resources. However, social assistance policy benefits are not originally or necessarily designed to assure older people live above the poverty threshold or avoid old age poverty risk (Nelson, 2012).

2.5 Summary and research gap

The literature part reviews the concept of poverty and poverty risk, present the role of welfare states and welfare state social policies programs to social inequality and poverty for citizens and older people. This dissertation's empirical countries are elected based on the Esping-Andersen's welfare states typology. Therefore, the above part gives and overview of his theoretical approach which presents how welfare states protect citizens from poverty and social inequality.

By explaining Esping-Andersen's definition of welfare states, the literature part also concludes his famous typology of welfare state regime. While this part also includes the critical debate of his approach. Under the analysis of the role of welfare state policies in old age, the literature part explains the role of welfare states for the poverty in old age as well as the other three social policy fields.

The results of the studies above have shown that pensions can be an effective tool to reduce vulnerability, inequality and poverty for older people. Long-term care is no longer defined or partly defined as informal family work in European welfare states, but as welfare state programs and resources (Long-term care benefits can somehow reduce old age poverty and support old age vulnerability in certain degrees). Social welfare programs such as social assistance system help to reduce poverty in various degrees in different countries. Studies which refer to policy fields of health and long-term care policy have made a contribution by describing and analyzing the changing institutional landscape of these policies and politics throughout Europe.

Overall, after discussions on various aspects of poverty and definition of poverty in literature, the concept of poverty in this dissertation follows a European Council decision of 1984 on targeted measures to combat poverty as it is more coherent to research methods in this dissertation. Therefore, older people are regarded as "impoverished" if they have such small means that they are excluded from the way of life in the member state. This concept of poverty is also based on the definition of the European Union poverty thresholds and the poverty definition which was recommended by the Statistic Office of the EU (Eurostat), but the targeted people in this dissertation are older people. Therefore, older people are considered to be at risk of poverty if their disposal income is less than 60% of the national median income.

However, on the basis of a theoretical poverty concept which only focuses on the impact of ageing policy for older people instead of all other material sources such as family transfer, this dissertation asks how ageing policies differ in their impact on poverty risk for older people in European welfare states. Ageing policy is of course not a new term in social science research, and it refers to many other policy fields in literature. For example, authors have done studies on ageing policy which refer to policy fields of health and long-term care by comparing policy situations among the EU, the OECD and the WHO, and made contributions by describing and analyzing the changing institutional landscape of these policies and politics throughout Europe (Ervik and Linden, 2013). It is found that "policy ideals in three organizations differ on the concept of 'active ageing' while they emphasize different aspect of 'healthy ageing' concerning their health and long-term care policy fields albeit three organizations all concern the preparation and services for older people." This result was found in the book *The Making of Ageing Policy: Theory and Practice in Europe* (Ervik and Lindén, 2013). In this book, authors focus on the need for policies addressing concerns about the future financing of pensions and health systems and the scarcity of labor, especially within the care sector, and these challenges and opportunities have increasingly been put on the agenda at various governance levels. The book analyzed policy ideas and practices at both international and the national levels and commented on the tension between official policies based on a "burden of dependency" assumption, as well as policies stressing the opportunities that came with longevity (Ervik and Linden, 2013). But the "ageing policy" concept in the book was restricted to health policy and long-term care policy which is different to the concept of "ageing policy" in this dissertation, since it does not consider the role of pension policy and policy towards social assistance.

So far, research about the systematic interaction of the interplay between different policy fields in their role for poverty risks of older people is still missing, as well as cross-national research about this question. How different policy fields interact in their role for the income situation of older people and to avoid poverty risk in older age, and how this differs in different types of welfare states, is still rarely studied. However, it would be important to analyze this in order to understand the relationship between welfare state policies and poverty in older age.

Chapter 3 Theoretical approach

3.1 General assumptions about the relationship between welfare state policies and poverty risk in older age

Paid work is the main basis for the social integration of the citizens of industrial and postindustrial societies and the main source for their income. After retirement, people are particularly vulnerable in their economic situation, since they are no longer able to live on an employment income. Therefore, the risk of poverty would strongly increase without welfare state support, particularly for the lower classes and middle classes (Budovski & Tillmann, 2006; Callan et al., 2008, p. 74). According to Callan, the "the volatility of the risk relates in part to the fact that many older people are heavily dependent on the state pension, either contributory or non-contributory. If these payment rates are close to the poverty threshold, a small change either way (or a small additional income) can move many older people above or below the threshold" (Callan et al., 2008, p. 74). If the state pension is above the poverty threshold, older people could be exposed to highly poverty risk directly. In addition, the way how family support older people has significant impact on their poverty condition. Therefore, the main stabilizator of older people living situation is pension income. A stabilized pension benefit provides older people with positive impact of financial difficulties and deteriorated health conditions. Public social services are also essential for the changing condition of the at-risk-of-poverty rate for older people.

In its general theoretical concept about the relationship between welfare state policies and poverty, this dissertation relates to the theoretical approach of Esping-Andersen (1990, 1999). Esping-Andersen theorizes the relationship between welfare state policies and poverty in his theoretical approach of the "welfare regimes" that he introduced in his book *The Three Worlds of Welfare Capitalism* of 1990. Esping-Andersen (1990) argues that the welfare state has an important role for the support of older people with an income and social services, and that welfare state policies are important for people's income situation in older age. Welfare states implement social policies to offer citizens social security and social services mainly also for those periods of their life in which they are not themselves able to earn their income from paid employment like in their life stage after the end of their working life. Welfare states offer them pensions for the life phase after retirement as a (more or less generous) substitute for their employment income, as well as payment for social services if they are in need of care. It should also be considered that pensions differ between social groups, for example between women and men. Men, in general, have better pensions. The reason is that in most postindustrial societies, women participate less in the labor market than men. Particularly in welfare states in which the pensions are work-related, like in the conservative type of welfare regime, this leads to lower pensions for women (Zaidi, Grech and Fuch, 2006).

However, it should be considered that welfare states do not determine the degree of poverty in older age in society. The reason is that people in part also have multiple income sources, like income transfers within the family, savings, assets, social benefits, earnings, public assistance, veteran's benefits and assistance under emergency situations, and fortune. This is also the reason why welfare state policies are more relevant for lower and middle income classes than for the highest income classes. This dissertation only focuses on the degree to which welfare state policies towards pension, long-term care and social assistance hypothetically cause poverty among older people if they do not have relevant additional resources.

Esping-Andersen has also pointed out that there are substantial differences with regard to the generosity of welfare states towards social security and social services. Therefore, it is plausible to assume that welfare states differ substantially with regard to the poverty risks that are related to their policies for older people (1990). According to Esping-Andersen's approach, particularly also the more generous social democratic welfare states do not only to guarantee basic living condition and establish basic the safety net for citizens, but they in part further de-commodify citizen's living condition in order to let them choose freely not to take market participation without worry about incomes.

3.2 Introduction of the theoretical concept of "Ageing Policy"

In this part, I introduce a theoretical approach concerning the role of welfare state policies for poverty risk of older people, the approach of the "ageing policy" that I have developed. It is argued that the common way to conceptualize the relationship between the welfare state and poverty of people in older age is too restricted. It was shown in the literature overview that it is common to argue that pension policies affect the degree of poverty risk in older age. There is also some research in connection with long-term care policies for older people. This dissertation argues that it is important to understand the interaction of (at least) three different types of policies in their role for poverty in old age, in order to explain how welfare states affect poverty in old age.

The approach of "Ageing Policy" stresses the role of each of three policies field for poverty risk for older people, pension policy, long-term care policy and social assistance policy, and also the way in which these policies interact in their framing of the income situation of older people.

Pensions are relevant for the income situation and how people make a living after retirement, long-term care is relevant for resources when they are in need of care, while social assistance is relevant for payment if people do not have relevant income sources in older age. These policy fields interact in ageing policy fields and are highly relevant for the risk of poverty in old age in welfare states. These policy fields have an integrated impact on poverty risk. One or two of them may be connected with poverty risks. In this case, the other policy/policies may compensate this so that the interaction of all three policies is not connected with poverty risks, or the poverty risk that is connected with one or two of these policies is not compensated.

The public pension system has an important role in protecting older people from poverty risks in European countries. In this system, minimum pension schemes are essential. The fixed amount of minimum pension guarantees older people a basic living standard which means when minimum pension benefit level is relatively high, older people may have less possibility to suffer poverty risk than in case the minimum pension is relatively low. For countries without minimum pension, older people's poverty risk depends on the regulation within the pension system about the conditions of access to the pension system, the conditions to receive full pensions and the generosity in the size of the pensions. In social insurance-based pension systems, which are based on people's income during their life course, people with low income often face high risks of older age poverty (Frericks, 2014). With the absence of public pension schemes, almost all European countries would be faced with a significantly higher poverty risk of older people.

Also, policies towards long-term care impact on poverty risk in older age.

The importance of care and health problems in late life has been amply studied in social gerontology as a cause of vulnerability (Schröder-Butterfill & Marianti, 2006). The World Health Organization (WHO, 2011) publishes the "Global Health and Aging" report, which investigates that the new patterns of older people's disease as "epidemiologic transition" which is characterized by the "waning of infectious and acute diseases and the emerging important of chronic and degenerative diseases" (WHO, 2011, p. 9). The long-term increase in the share of older people with dementia, especially Alzheimer's disease even increases older people's risk to become care-dependent in older age. Social care benefit and services in welfare state policies towards health care and long-term care have a strong impact on poverty risk for older people, particularly when people have a high level of care need. Older people face poverty if they are experiencing lower levels of social care services or cannot receive sufficient care benefits from the state (Chou & Kröger, 2008, 2010).

If older people are in need of long-term care and public resources would not be available, they would be dependent on care by family members and their savings. For a long time in industrial society, care by female family members was the main source for long-term care. However, because women's employment has increased, family care is much less available. Also, savings of people with low incomes during their life course and people with strong care needs most often are not high enough to pay for long-term care. When older people can hardly reach long-term care resources or they must exhaust their own resources in order to reach long-term care policy resource, they will face increased poverty risk in countries with low public support for long-term care. When public support for long-term care is comprehensively available and covers all care needs, this policy field is generous and helps to avoid poverty risk in the older age.

Social assistance programs have been regarded to reduce poverty risk to a certain degree. They have usually been devised to supplement people's basic living needs and costs, and provide a minimum social protection standard in practice. However, social assistance benefit standards may differ across welfare states, and they may be below or above the poverty level in different countries. The differences are high in this regard among European countries (European Parliament, 2009).

The focus of this dissertation is restricted to the ways in which the three types of policy hypothetically contribute to poverty risk in old age, therefore, I use the term of "poverty risk for older people". The definition of poverty on which dissertation is based, on the one hand, follows a European Council decision of 1984 which was on the target to combat poverty, on the other hand, it is also based on the definition of European Union and thresholds recommended by the Statistic Office of the EU (Eurostat). However, the definition of poverty in this dissertation is not the same as real poverty in reality; instead this dissertation only focuses on the degree to which welfare state policies towards pensions, long-term care and social assistance hypothetically cause poverty among older people if they do not have additional resources.

This dissertation develops a theoretical typology of different types of ageing policy based on different ways in which ageing policies impact on poverty risk for older people in different types of welfare states. A typology is characterized as a "theoretical typology" in comparative sociology, if it is based on theoretical assumptions about relations between different variables, which is the case in this typology. An "empirical typology" would in contrast construct the different types on the basis of the empirical material of a study .

This typology is based on two dimensions that indicate the generosity level of each country's ageing policy fields, explained as dimension A: eligibility requirements before an individual access to benefits, B: size of benefit in the degree to which individual could access.

Based on these dimensions, different country's ageing policy generosity levels are distinguished. They are called here: "poverty less protected model" "poverty more protected model" and "poverty medium protected model". The different types can be described as follows.

The "poverty less protected model" of ageing policy is based on the interplay between the three policy fields in which at least one policy field does not avoid poverty. Also, this is not compensated by another policy field. For example, it is possible that pension policy does not avoid poverty, but social assistance for older people is also below the poverty level, the state does not avoid poverty.

The "poverty more protected model" is designed so that the welfare state in each of the three policy fields is generous, and all policy fields do avoid poverty in older age.

The "poverty medium protected model" of "Ageing Policy" is based on the interplay between the three policy fields in which at least one policy field does not avoid poverty. However, this is compensated by anther policy field. It is for example possible, that pension policy does not avoid poverty, but social assistance is above the poverty level and therefore, the lack of protection against poverty risk in the pension system is compensated by the social assistance system.

3.3 Main assumptions related to the explanation of cross-national differences in the poverty risks in the context of "Ageing Policies"

The main assumption of this dissertation is that different types of ageing policies differ in their impacts on avoiding poverty risk for older people in European welfare states. I compare ageing politics on the basis of the degree of generosity of each single policy field and of the whole field of ageing policy. The dissertation is based on the theoretical assumption that cross-national differences in ageing policies between welfare states can be explained with the welfare regime typology of Esping-Andersen (1990, 1999). According to this theoretical approach, it is possible to distinguish (at least) three different types of welfare regimes.

The “liberal” type of welfare regime has ideal typically a means-tested social assistance system and modest universal social transfer system. Their social benefits level is very modest and strictly restricted to needy people. This type of welfare states has minimized the de-commodification effects. Social benefits cannot prevent people from being exposed to poverty risks. The access procedures to social benefits are often related with social stigma.

I assume that in these countries, not all ageing policy fields help to avoid poverty risk for older people and they partly affect each other. The interplay among ageing policy fields is not complementary and each policy field contributes to poverty risk. When one policy field contributes to poverty risk for older people, other policy fields cannot compensate the gap or contributes to more gaps to poverty risk. The risk for old age poverty on the basis of ageing policy is high.

The second cluster is “conservative” welfare regime. Ideal typically in this type, social rights are attached to social status and states have replaced the market to provide social insurance and social welfare. The state will interfere until their own resources are exhausted. People’s social benefits are very closely related with social insurance which means people’s performance and contribution to the insurance in their working life is crucial for their social benefits level. Better work performance with higher income, longer contribution period to social insurance will buy them less chance to be exposed to poverty risk. However, gender inequality has a strong effect in this cluster of countries since women are not encouraged to participate in the labor market in the traditional conservative countries.

I assume that in these welfare states, all ageing policy fields may contribute to the poverty risk for older people but they incompletely compensate with each other. Here the interplay among ageing policy fields is partly complementary. When one ageing policy field leaves a gap to poverty risk, other policy fields incompletely fill this gap, and the risk for old age poverty on the basis of ageing policy is medium. The last type of countries is the "social democratic regime type". In this type, the state takes full responsibility to take care of older people, children and needy people with direct social transfers to them. These countries have the highest standard of equality. Social benefits are not to meet citizen's basic or minimized needs, but to satisfy the upgraded needs. This type of welfare states system protects citizens from being exposed to poverty risks.

I assume that in these countries, all policy fields help to avoid poverty risk for older people. The interplay among ageing policy fields is complementary. In principle, each policy field prevents poverty risk for older people. When one policy field fails to protect older people from being exposed to poverty risk, other policy fields will back up completely and that the risk for old age poverty on the basis of Ageing Policy is low.

Chapter 4 Methodological approach

4.1 Measurement of poverty risk

Poverty risk is measured within social welfare policy fields of pension, long-term care and social assistance policy. I make general poverty risk measurement based on ageing policy fields' main features, policy access principles, policy benefits and generosity conditions. By comparing the generosity condition of each empirical country's ageing policy fields and analyzing policy fields' inner relationship, this dissertation presents the theoretical poverty risk condition for older people. The focus of this dissertation is restricted to the ways in which the three types of policy hypothetically contribute to theoretical poverty risk in the old age. Therefore, I use the term of "theoretical poverty risk for older people".

To prevent any misleading, it should be clear that the poverty condition I try to measure is the hypothetical condition. The measurement of poverty is based on the poverty definition in the dissertation which is focused only on older people. As it has mentioned above, measurement of poverty in this dissertation is not the same as real poverty in reality with its own limitations. Since older people have widely sources of benefits and incomes, such as pension, capital assets, relative supports, social benefits, earnings, public assistance, etc., it is hard to measure all kinds of their income and benefits source, instead, I only introduce older people's income and benefits from welfare regime policies. Therefore, this dissertation only focuses on the degree to which welfare state policies towards pension, long-term care and social assistance policy hypothetically cause poverty among older people if they do not have additional resources. Therefore, the definition of poverty is a theoretical concept referred to as "poverty risk for older people". Besides, low incomes in comparison with other residents in different countries do not show strict signs of the low living standard.

4.2 Cross-national comparative approach and explanation of selection of countries

This dissertation is based on a comparative study of three European welfare states, which represent the different types of welfare regimes in Esing-Andersen's theoretical approach. Germany represents the conservative welfare regime, Denmark represents the Social Democratic welfare regime and the UK represents the liberal welfare regime. The aim is to evaluate the theoretical assumptions about the differences in the ageing policies in different types of welfare states which were introduced in 4.3.

This part gives a short overview of the ageing policies of the three countries.

Social democratic welfare states are characterized by "promoting an equality of the highest standards, not equality of minimal needs as was pursued elsewhere. Services and benefits are updated to levels commensurate with even the most discriminating tastes of the new middle classes", by Esping-Andersen (1990, p. 27). These welfare states encourage individual independence, address the comprehensive ideal between family and market, and employ the states' role as a safety line.

The situation in the UK is described by Esping-Andersen (1990) as where "the state encourages the market, either positively guaranteeing only a minimum or actively subsidizing private welfare schemes. Benefits are typically modest, and entitlement rules are strict and often associated with stigma" (p. 26).

Conservative welfare states like Germany are characterized by "strongly committing to the preservation of traditional familyhood" (Esping-Anderson, 1990, p. 27). However, the German welfare state has strongly extended social rights and infrastructure in the field of elderly care with relatively generous long-term care policies (Ostner and Mätzke, 2013; Pfau-Effinger et al., 2014). The German retirement income act (Alterseinkünftegesetz) was introduced in 2005, and the German pension system also partially has characteristics of the type found in a liberal political economy (Bridgen and Mayer, 2014).

The German "long-term care insurance act" was introduced in 1995 and 1996, and long-term care responsibility for older people was defined as a task for the central German state. Until 2017, Germen long-term care insurance benefit has creased and assessment standards have been modified to five very detailed care grades follow by a complex coring system. German social assistance system has had a positive role as "back up policy" in framing poverty risk for older people but not enough. The non-contributory, means-tested social assistance policy field will still not take effect until families are short of resources.

Denmark's social policy has also changed since the early 1990s. Danish spending on social protection is among the highest in Europe and its spending on benefits and support for older people is much higher than in most European countries. Through reforms,

Denmark has raised taxes to release the budget burden on social benefit spending, but it still has a strong pension system for old people with a guaranteed fixed amount of pension which is even higher than the old age income tax threshold (Danmarks Statistik, 2015a). Moreover, Denmark has developed an even more universalistic long-term care system with strong infrastructure and the most extensive and decentralized long-term care services and benefits for senior citizens. Of course, following the traditional rules, the Danish welfare state takes over the practical and financial responsibly of elderly care. The long-term care situation in Denmark is more favorable with less pressure than the other two countries examined in this dissertation. In addition, with a generous social assistance policy, this single policy field can cover the basic costs of living for older people.

The UK social welfare policy has changed many times and the UK has gone through a prolonged period of financial crisis and stagnation. According to many indicators, the UK economy has recovered somehow but the social benefits for older people are still low such as the new state pension. Besides, the long-term care and social assistance system in UK are both means-tested. The infrastructure and benefits have been extended over recent years, but the level of benefits has not increased meaningfully, so that they now hardly support older people from avoiding poverty risk.

4.3 The main dimensions of the comparative policy analysis for the single policy field

To compare single policy fields of ageing policies across countries, I refer to the criteria which Esping-Andersen (1990) introduced in his welfare regime approach to operationalizing the generosity of social right (pension, sickness insurance and unemployment benefits). He examined the rules of access to benefits (eligibility and restrictions on entitlements, such as contribution record and needs tests), the level of income replacement which was offered, and the range of entitlements (Esping-Andersen, 1990). I use two dimensions which are described as D. a: eligibility requirements before an individual access to benefits (restrictions of access), and D. b: size of benefit in the degree to which individual could access to analyze different generosity levels of ageing policy in different countries. The same single policy field in each country is measured under these dimensions and generosity conditions are shown to describe the comparison of the generosity of ageing policy.

To measure hypothetical impacts of ageing policy on poverty, this dissertation analyzes the question of how far ageing policy fields hypothetically prevent old age poverty risk on the basis of a poverty threshold. It compares spaces that each ageing policy field leaves to theoretical individual poverty risk for senior citizens in different regimes of European welfare states. A theoretical typology of countries based on their ageing policy's impact in preventing poverty risk for older people is shown.

4.4 Measurement of ageing policy as interaction of policy fields

In this part, I introduce how I measure ageing policies for the comparative study. Ageing policy in each country is a package which contains pension, long-term care and social assistance policy.

Since each policy field leaves spaces for poverty risk for older people, I analyze how far other policy fields compensate for these poverty risks or contribute to more poverty risks and present reasons. All policy fields are measured under the current policy schemes. It should be emphasized that what is innovative with regard to the method is that I measure the poverty risks of older people on the basis of analysis of the political institutions and regulation, and I do not measure poverty itself in the common way by using data about the actual poverty rates of older people in the population. It is a new type of measurement of social policies. But I also introduce different indicators related to the actual share of poor people.

Since many countries keep adjusting social welfare policies, such as Germany which has again on 1st January, 2018 increased long-term care benefit levels, the time dimension will also be considered, especially for pension measurement. It should also be considered that actual data about pension levels are the result of previous pension policy. For example, the UK basic state pension and additional state pension have been integrated into a whole piece as new state pension since the beginning of 2017, and benefit levels have comparatively increased. However, since each new pension scheme has a start year, older people who were born before that year have to stay with the old scheme. This limitation shows that the analysis of hypothetical poverty and inequality connected with a specific pension policy is particularly useful.

In Germany, each of three policy fields cause poverty risk for older people but they incompletely compensate with each other. The social assistance policy can only pay at the low level. Therefore it cannot completely compensate for poverty that is caused either by pension policies or long-term care policies or both. The poverty risk condition relies on the pension policy field in this country. Pensions as a main old age income source in German is a crucial factor which affects the poverty risk condition for older people. While Danish ageing policy picture has the overall function of preventing poverty risk. All policy fields help to avoid and eliminate poverty. Danish social assistance policy is also generous theoretically protect senior citizens from poverty risk. However, ageing policy in the UK is less generous compare with the other two countries. Pension benefits in the UK partly contribute to preventing older people from poverty risk while the UK long-term care policy field can also eliminate parts of poverty risk, but not the whole picture. Not all policy fields help to avoid poverty risk for older people and they partly affect each other but their joined effects do not prevent poverty risk for older people in this country.

4.5 Conclusion

The methodological part describes the concept of poverty and poverty risk of this dissertation as well as limitations of these measurements.

This part also introduces the methodological approach to the comparative analysis of ageing policies in different welfare states. The three countries of the study are selected based on the Esping-Andersen's typology of welfare regime. This part also gives a short overview of the development of the ageing policies of the three countries after Esping-Andersen has introduced his theoretical approach of the different "welfare regimes". It shows that all of these countries still more or less match with the classification in Esping-Andersen's typology.

The dimensions for comparing single policies in each country's ageing policy fields are also introduced. It is also introduced how the interaction of the interaction of the three ageing policy fields is analyzed. However, the limitation of this part is that I only include three welfare state in Europe, more countries and more policy fields should be included as well, especially housing and health policy fields which hopefully will become my future work.

In the next part, I will present the findings of the cross-national analysis of differences in ageing policies and poverty risk, which include each policy features, their generosity conditions, benefit levels and restrictions for older people in each country. And show overall pictures of each country's theoretical poverty situation under the effects of ageing policy.

Chapter 5 Cross-national differences in ageing policy and poverty risk

The generous condition of ageing policy varies across the three countries. Germany has the insurance-based ageing policy, and most benefits are relevant to the income-need assessment. Denmark has a universal, coherent and service-oriented ageing policy. The UK has a relatively narrow ageing policy with relatively low levels of benefits and services, and most of its ageing policy benefits depend on strict needs assessment. This part of the dissertation shows different generosity condition of ageing policies and hypothetical poverty in three countries

5.1 Poverty risk in old age in Germany

In this part, I analyze the poverty risk in the German welfare state by analyzing each policy field in the ageing policy package. For each policy field, I introduce their main features, access principles, policy benefits and generosity conditions. The analysis of the interaction of German ageing policy fields is presented in the end.

5.1.1 Pension policy

5.1.1.1 Main features

German now has a three-pillar pension system with the more typical of the combination of conservative and liberal policy economy. The first and the most important pillar is the public social insurance, or we call it Germany's public state pension, which is a mandatory, statutory and highly earns the oriented pension. As the OECD report (2016) emphases that German public state pension scheme is an earning-related point system on the basis of the pay-as-you-go model. Pension points are calculated through people's whole working career, which will be translated to pension benefits after retirement. The amount of the pension depends primarily on the wages and earnings that are insured by contributions. The value of a contribution period depends on the relationship between the annual gross salary and the average salary of all insured persons.

Contributions and rights are only for employed people with some re-distribution elements of family support. To receive a basic public pension, besides potential pension recipients making contributions to pension insurance during their working life, they also need to reach the normal pension age and complete the minimum qualifying period (insurance period). (Federal Statistic of Germany, European Statistic). The latest available retirement age in Germany is 65 for older people born before 1947 and 67 for older people born after 1964. For those who were born between 1947 and 1964, calculating retirement age is a bit complicated. For people born after 1947 the retirement age increase one month for every year until 1958 according to the law passed in 2007. For those born after 1958, the retirement age increases two months by each following year until it reaches 67 as the same of people born after 1964. In July 2014, there was a special length of service pension available for workers with 45 years of contributions when reaching the age of 63, but this special pension age increased until it reaches 65 in the year 2028. The final pension size is based on income substitute. Additional means-tested basic retirement in old age (Grundsicherung im Alter) from the social assistance policy field is regarded as minimum pension in German. German pension and social assistance policy fields have compensation at this point. The second pillar is the occupational pension which usually acts as a compensation arrangement for senior citizens, and can be granted by employers. About 50 per cent of all workers belong to these schemes. The third pillar of the pension system is the personal funded pension which is the market-based insurance system such as private pension schemes. These funds are protected by law and cannot be sized by the state. Benefits are completely dependent on the size of contributions. There are other new pensions (or new allowance for additional old-age provision) such as the Riester pension, and the Ruerup pension are provided in 2018. But these allowances are excluded from the statutory pension insured recipients.

5.1.1.2 Pension benefits

According to pension pillars designed above, the actual benefits levels of German pension in the federal retirement system is directly related to the amount of income and contribution throughout the whole career. The general rule is, the higher the income during a working career, the larger amount paid directly to the national retirement funds over decades should be, and the higher payment older people can receive after retirement. But those who earned less and paid less to the pension system or made fewer pension contributions than 35 years can only receive a lower pension even below the poverty level. Most people rely on public pensions heavily after retirement. But since 2007, the third pillar pension (funded pension plans) have increased while households that rely on public pensions have decreased. However, the success of the regulated personal pension market still contains considerable doubt, and the occupational system is in decline (Willert, 2011; Hagen and Kleinlein, 2012).

The average old-age income is around 50% of the national average income. The first and second pillar pensions are paid out depending on how much people contribute and for how long. According to German pension regulations, the exact amount is calculated:

"*... based on total individual earnings points multiplied by the pension factor of* 1.0 *and the pension value. Individual earnings points are calculated as individual annual earnings divided by the average earnings of all contributors multiplied by the entry factor. The pension value is calculated as the monthly benefit amount for One year of average covered earnings, adjusted according to changes in wages*" (*SSPTW*, 2016, *p*. 119).

Unlike Denmark, there is no guaranteed minimum statuary pension in Germany. In addition, a shift of pension taxation further reduces pension payments. The retirement income act (Alterseinkünftegesetz) was introduced in 2005, and all forms of pensions started from the statuary pension scheme gradually carried over to full taxation until 2040 (DRV, 2010). Therefore, all old age pension benefits which are above the basic pension threshold have been included in pensioners' individual income tax rate. But at the same time, tax allowance is also included in this pension taxation so that double taxation can be avoided. Nevertheless, pensions are always below the basic pension threshold if there is no other source of income for senior citizens.

5.1.1.3 Access principles to pensions

Germany pension policy scheme is high insurance based, theoretically, everyone who has made contributions is under the protection of the pension insurance system. However, the exact pension amount paid to older people is different. If they get the full pension, they have to make the full period of pension contribution at the full amount and reach pension age. Family supports to older people has its strong traditional role in Germany, which embodies its effects in various forms, such as widow pension, monetary support, food and daily staff support, etc. Widow pension (window's pension from the statutory pension insurance) is one of the important and effective family supports for older people. To access this pension, the deceased must be a pensioner at the time of death and fulfil the general waiting period.

Early retirement is possible in Germany, but the pension benefit will be relatively reduced by 0.3 per cent each month before pensioners reach their normal pension age. A deferred retirement is encouraged by increasing relative 0.5 V.H. of pension benefit each month after the normal pension age for longer workers. Pension assessment is based on individual conditions, when pension contribution was interrupted by care work, family caregivers can receive pension credits in the form of paid contributions by long-term care insurance to the statutory pension insurance. These caregivers must have provided unpaid care work for at least

14 hours per week with care giving allowance and do not have other extra paid employment more than 30 hours per week. When parents care for the child younger than three years, they can receive pension credits, when parents have at least 25 years of contributions and give care work for the child under ten years; the additional years are credited if parents work part-time. These additional credited years can work for the same situation but parents who do not work because of caring to at least two children under ten years old. What I find on the limitation of these pension access principles is "time difference". Pension benefits and contribution regulations are adjusted annually, new pension policy schemes are introduced gradually; however, every new adjustment or policy scheme has a start date. People who were born before that date have to continue their benefits under the old policy scheme. Therefore, different age groups among older people are receiving the pension under different benefit schemes. Thus, may deteriorate income and living condition of the much older people who are having worse health condition than the other younger groups.

5.1.1.4 Generosity level of pension policy field

The average income of all insured persons is determined by the Federal Government with the consent of the Federal Council. When we check the data collected by the Federal Statistic Office, the average income is set at 36.187 Euros in 2016, and for the year 2017 is 37.103 Euros, and for the year 2018, it is around 37.873 Euros. Generally, German pension is in principle around 50 per cent of the average income accounted by contribution and credit points. But this amount is only for those who have full employment age and full employment time. Most women do not have full-time employment because of care work. Although long-term care insurance contribution to the statutory pension pillar and care allowance, the actual pension lose exist in between due to long-term care insurance limitation on care hours and paid employment.

German standard pension is about 1,284.06 Euros (1,230.34 Euros in East Germany) in 2018. But the standard pension is linked to "certain events in the employment biography (45 years, average income, etc.)(§ 154 Abs. 3 Satz 1 Nr. 2 SGB Ⅵ) which is higher than German average pension. The average monthly pension is about 1,100 Euros in 2017, but in many cases, the retirees can get much less. The German net pension replacement rate is around 51 per cent for the average earner which below the average figure of OECD as 63 per cent according to OECD statistic (OECD, 2017). And this is just on the average level. For those low earners whose net replacement rate is as 55 per cent, fall much lower than the OECD average level as 73 per cent. Since German minimum pension is at very low level with restricted benefit period, and minimum pension benefit belongs to social assistance policy field but not comes from pension policy field itself, German pension system itself produces a relatively high share of potential poverty risk for older people, especially for women who did not work in the standard employment relationship or even if they did so, their low-income is not to secure themselves from exposing to potential poverty risks after retirement. According to OECD statistics, currently, German women are suffering the largest gender pension gap compare among OECD countries as 46 per cent. Besides, the large share of women taking part-time job currently which means those women's pension in the old age will be dragged down even much more than men shortly. German pension policies have been changed over years, and so-called flexible pension reforms have been introduced in recent years. Some studies have suggested that these flexible pension reforms could increase earlier retirement scheme. But new pension benefits do not have much impact on improving low pensioner's income condition. Because the low-income old people have to reply on old age safety net such as a basic retirement benefit, whose benefit level is relatively low as around 20 per cent of average earning (around 681 Euros per month if we consider the data from 2017) from social assistance system. Therefore, older people who worked as partial careers and low-income pensioners face comparatively serious possibility to expose to theoretical poverty risks.

The principle for the generosity of pension policies is based on two dimensions: eligibility requirements before an individual access to benefits, and size of benefit in the degree to which individual could access. The basic public pension generosity is compared with the "at-risk-of-poverty threshold" which was set to 60 per cent of the national equalized median income. German at-risk-of-poverty threshold is 12,707 Euros in 2016 and 12,729 Euros in 2017 (EU-SILC survey, Eurostat, 2018), which equals to monthly 1,058 Euros and 1,060 Euros in the recent two years. However, in the year 2017, the German average pension is very close to this poverty threshold, but the real condition is many retirees' pension benefits cannot reach to this average level, while low-income old people who rely on old age safety net or the basic retirement benefit can only get approximately less than 700 Euros per month.

Based on this analysis, German older people have a real big problem of being exposed to potential poverty risk because of low pension benefits and low level of minimum pension. Older people are able to reach the basic benefits in the old age (Grundsicherung im Alter) when they are considered as poor people and other resources have exhausted, but eligibility roles are strictly. This mean-tested basic benefit in the old age is the German minimum pension. But it is granted only for 12 months normally (with exceptional cases in which benefit period could be extended longer) with fixed amount of 416 Euros in 2018 at its highest level (Regelbedarfsstufe 1) (§ 28 SGB Ⅻ). However, theoretically, this the old age basic benefit is a part of social assistance, it does not even belong to German pension system. When considering household-based pension in Germany, it is not so bad as individual pension condition which makes Germany older people really poor. Living in couples makes women old age pension better when their husbands earn enough. But for most women themselves only get very low pension income or the basic retirement benefit or do not have the basic retirement benefit. However, after the death of husbands, the widow does not have enough pension benefit to protect themselves from being exposed to potential high poverty risks. Actually, within the German pension system, the part-time job and financial break made older people poorer. Even with a low level of pension and minimum pension, older people still face poverty risks. Therefore, the pension system itself does not avoid poverty in German for older people.

5.1.2 Long-term care policy

5.1.2.1 Main features

Esping-Andersen (1990) has concluded that social insurance reproduces social inequality for long-term care field because only employed people have rights to cover their expenses under social insurance social model. However, German has the different character as a highly social insurance-oriented society. In German, only employed people pay contributions to long-term care insurance, but all citizens have long-term care benefits under the long-term care insurance regulations, even for those who do not make contributions.

The long-term care system is a public-insurance system in Germany which contributes to the needy and pensioners contribute themselves. It includes social long-term care insurance and private long-term care insurance, which together cover almost the whole population who are enrolled in the Statutory Health Insurance (GKV) according to the principle "the long-term care insurance follows the health insurance". Public covers 90% of the population, and private long-term care insurances, which covers 10% of the population, both as compulsory insurance. As private care insurance is highly selective and has an income threshold, it was excluded from this dissertation.

5.1.2.2 Long-term care benefits

Public long-term care in Germany is now delivered as home care and residential care. A care allowance is paid if older people choose a family member to provide care services. The care allowance is low and is not paid directly to the family care giver, but to the care recipients. Home care benefits are from €125 monthly (CG1) to €316 monthly (CG2) to €545 monthly (CG3) to €728 monthly (CG4) and €901 monthly (CG5) [Zweites Pflegestärkungsgesetz (PSG Ⅱ)]. This detail means that the care grade one includes those people who do not need any specific support but require "long-term care counselling". Benefit from care grade two to care grade five can basically cover recipients' long-term care costs but not all. Replacement care benefits are available if a family caregiver is on a break from work, in part-time work, or on holiday. The long-term care insurance covers the costs of replacement care from another family caregiver or care agency. The amount is possible for up to 4 weeks and €1,612 yearly for all care grades (§ 45b SGB Ⅺ). If older people are in need of home care service, long-term care insurance covers support services which should be delivered at a particular daily period. Payments are from €689 monthly (CG2) to 1.298 (CG3) to €1.612 (care CG4), and €1,995 is guaranteed monthly to care grade five cases since 2016 (§ 45b SGB Ⅺ) (details are shown in Appendix 2). This part of care benefit covers care cost, about 76% of older people who receive long-term care choose home care rather than agency care in 2016 (Bundesministerium for Gesundheit, 2016) (details shown in Appendix 4).

Concerning residential care, the size of care benefits covers old recipients in all care grades. Care insurance paid amount varies according to the extent of the individual's requirements. Part-time day and night residential care services are paid the same as home care service. Full-time residential care service supports older people if they stay in residential households, i.e., a nursing home. A lump sum of €125 (CG1), €770 (CG2), €1.262 (CG3) to €1.775 (CG4) and €2.005 (CG5) is guaranteed monthly from 2016 (§ 45a SGB Ⅺ) (detailed in Table 3). But residential care only covers the care costs, co-payment costs, the accommodation costs and food are not included, however, these parts of costs are extremely high for older people. After the reform in 2017, co-payment for residential care has been set as a fixed amount with no longer increase with rising care needs for care recipients who are assigned from care grade two to five, but the exact amount is different from one care homes to another. The accommodation cost is applied to investment cost while there is no subsidizes. Nevertheless, German social assistance covers parts of these accommodation and housing costs for older people. Moreover, senior citizens can decide on home care or residential care, or forward parts or all of the funds to family caregivers, but they cannot choose particular family members.

5.1.2.3 Access principles

German long-term care policy's access principle is designed based on the needs-tested scheme. Under the acts of 2015, the assessment procedure before approaching benefits serves to measure a person's physical health condition. But later in August 2015, the Federal Cabinet passed the Second Bill to strengthen long-term care, which was scheduled to be introduced in January 2016. A new assessment procedure as well as the changes in the benefit amount available to recipients of the long-term care insurance entered into force from January 2017 (Germany Federal Minister of Health, 2017). According to this Bill, the amount of long-term care benefit is determined by what older people can still do on their own and on which part assistance is still needed. The great change is that these care needs are no longer concern whether the need arises because of dementia or because of physical frailty. In this way, all persons in need of long-term care will have equal access to the benefits provided by the long-term care insurance (Germany Federal Minister of Health, 2016). The access principles for disabled older people include disabilities both in physical, in mental health and cognition and include social factors. Under the new act, all kinds of self-reliance restrictions are taken into account.

All these measures collect potential long-term care recipients into care grades which largely widens the number of the older people who are going to have long-term care benefits and services for the first time or who are in the lower level of long-term care needs. Before the implementation of the Second Bill, formal regulations stated that "old people only have the right to receive paid care if they can prove that they have a physical need for it through illness or disability" (§ 14 Abs. 1 SGB Ⅺ). For those older people who are already included by a care allowance and care benefits through passing strict selection criteria, if they are not seriously ill, long-term care only covers their physical healthcare needs. Other aspects of care except for actual physical health, they must organize by themselves (Pfau-Effinger, Hensen, Och, 2011). However, all persons in need of long-term care now have equal access to the benefits provided by long-term care insurance even at the early stage, and housework assistance can also be supported. From this point of view, some of the family caring burdens can be relieved to some extent. Nevertheless, recipients still rely on support from family members if they are willing to live in their household or rely on people outside their family, such as their social network if these people accept the conditions on care work that are done by family members (Statistisches Bundesamt, 2015) (details are also shown in Table 1). This new long-term care system is relatively complex, especially concerning the assessment measures, scoring points and the transparent problems for both former long-term care recipients as well as potential care recipients.

Now five valid care grades have replaced the three previous care categories of the German care system. These five care grades equally include physical, mental and psychological impairments, and all potential care recipients can reach assessment process by applications. There is no longer any need to make a distinction between physical and mental restrictions such as dementia as the former system did (Germany Federal Minister of Health, 2015). The assessment serves to measure and evaluate the degree of a person's independence in six different areas independently: mobility (10%), cognitive and communication skills, behavior and psychological problems (all together is 15%), self-care (40%), ability to cope with and independent handling of demands and pressures caused by illness or the need for therapy (20%), and organizing everyday life and social contacts (15%). This new system also gives weight points to each area in order to measure potential recipients' long-term care needs. The point value is between 0 (the person can carry out the activity without a helping person, but only with the use of aids) as a rule to 3 (the person cannot perform the activity, not even in parts). Afterwards, the points with different weightings are combined to form a total value, which stands for five care grades. From 12.5 to 27 points for care grade one (minor impairments of autonomy or of skills), from 27 to 47.5 points for care grade two (considerable impairments of autonomy or of skills), from 47.5 to 70 points for care grade three (serious impairments of autonomy or of skills), from 70～90 points for care grade four (severe impairments of autonomy or of skills), and from to 90 to 100 points for the last care grade (most severe impairments of autonomy or of skills) (Germany Federal Minister of Health, 2017).

This new assessment measurement is rather detailed but also very complex. In addition, it shows that the threshold to assessment grades is relatively low and cannot show the effective function of each assessment area. Take "mobility" as an example, it weighs only 10% in maximum in the assessment measurement process, but has 12.5～27 points when scoring the assessment (details are also shown in Table 2).

5.1.2.4 Generosity level of long-term care policy field

The generosity level of German long-term care is compared with covering long-term care needs by itself regardless of other welfare social policies. Analysis of long-term care policy is based on the assumption that policy itself covers overall long-term care needs of older people with full consideration of generosity dimensions. When long-term care resources are reachable and cover overall care needs, this policy field is generous and helps to avoid poverty risk in the older age. When long-term care policy field can cover necessary care needs or only parts of care needs, poverty risk will appear. When older people can hardly reach long-term care resources, or they must exhaust their own resources in order to reach long-term care policy resource, they will face poverty risk.

After the new reform recently, the German long-term care policy benefits are more comprehensive and generous than before. Advisory service consultants are available to people in need of care and family members (§7a SGB Ⅺ). People who apply for benefits or who already receive benefits are entitled to free individual care advice. Long-term care insurance is obliged to name of an advisor with special care advice training who can provide care help to any request. And long-term care insurance will make an appointment to individual care consultation with two weeks after care recipients make applications. This new long-term care consultants service is closer to the characteristics of Denmark long-term care services, which will make care services more coherent. However, the gap of between German long-term care policy resources and poverty risk mainly exist in the institutional care. In this care case, older people are less interested in the amount of cash benefit, but more interested in the care-related costs that they have to pay. Under the new regulation, the fixed amount of co-payments is 587 Euros at the federal average level from care grade two to five (Germany Federal Minister of Health, 2017). However, the specific amount various by different care homes, some could be much higher. Moreover, accommodation costs and food care excluded from long-term care benefits. People in need of long-term care have to bear these expensive costs by themselves, which exposed older people to poverty risks.

After all, the German welfare state has a more comprehensive care provision now, most of the long-term care resources are reachable, but the policy system exists leaks in covering care needs for older people especially in the residential care part. Which means in principal, long-term care services situation there can better protect frail older people from poverty than before but still leave gaps to older age poverty risk.

5.1.3 Social assistance policy

German social assistance provides services for those citizens who are unable to cover their needs with own resources and without those necessary resources from other social security system like pension system. It includes a non-contributory, means-tested system for senior citizens who fall on hard times. It is in the form of services, benefit payments and benefits in kind (Federal ministry of labour and social affairs, July 2011). It is the task of social assistance "to enable the beneficiaries to lead a life that corresponds to the dignity of man” (§ 1 Satz 1 SGB Ⅻ).

The generosity level of social assistance policy field is compared with the national’s poverty threshold with full consideration of generosity dimensions. The analysis of social assistance policy is based on the assumption that social assistance policy itself covers the living costs of older people.

In principle, in the case of insufficient income, German social assistance policy field covers the decent subsistence level. But in many cases, older people need to provide the necessary evidence to reach social assistance such as when they need social assistance benefit for long-term care costs. Therefore, a central principle of this social assistance system is to strengthen self-help and self-independency as explained in the SGB Ⅻ that “the service should enable as much as possible to live independently of it; the beneficiaries have to work to their best”(§ 1 Satz 2 SGB Ⅻ). Hence, social assistance services can only be provided after all of the people’s other options have been exhausted, for example, use out of the beneficiary’s own income and assets and financial support from family.

In the point of compensation for pension policy, senior citizens could continue to receive social assistance towards living expenses or means-tested basic benefits in old age (Grundsicherung im Alter) when they reach standard retirement age (§ 41-46b SGB Ⅻ). This benefit is calculated in the assistance to living and are usually granted for 12 months in cash benefit priority over non-cash benefit such as service and contribution in kind (§ 10 SGB Ⅻ). The benefit amounts are calculated as fixed amount according to requirement level 2 and level 3 (Regelbedarfsstufe). Unlike other social assistance services and benefits, the basic retirement benefit has to be applied and will not start immediately once the social assistance institution considered the recipients' conditions are met. (§ 18 in conjunction with § 41 SGB Ⅻ). The access principle towards its assessment measure is about income situation both from older people themselves and family members. The basic benefit in old age (Grundsicherung im Alter) is provided to both pension insured old people and non-insured older people. But this benefit level cannot secure old people being exposed to theoretical poverty risk. Nevertheless, it helps those non-insured old people a bit to improve living conditions even though it cannot get started at once since they need.

Besides, concerning the theoretical poverty risk exist in the long-term care policy field for older people, Germany social assistance policy field somehow compensate this leak by accommodation cost compensation. According to the general principle of the social assistance system, "the costs for accommodation and heating are always provided in the amount of the actual expenses, as far as they are appropriate (SGB Ⅻ)". "The job centre is geared to the local level of rents in the housing market (SGB Ⅻ)." But If accommodation in the amount of reasonable rental costs is considered "unreasonably high", they are to be provided as long as a change to a cheaper apartment is not possible or reasonable(regularly a maximum of 6 months) (§ 35 SGB Ⅻ). However, this accommodation compensation is made to people's living hood. SGB Ⅻ also set a benefit limit equal to other family members and the cost of accommodation. Maintenance entitlements of long-term care (apart from a few exceptions) are transferred in a flat-rate amount to the social assistance institution, up to a maximum of 32.75 (§ 70-74 SGB Ⅻ) for care assistance. The amounts are determined by the "Laender". And there is no recourse regularly for the basic benefits in old age. Moreover, on the basis of a principle in the social assistance policy filed that beneficiaries have to use their own assets first until their resources are exhausted, expensive accommodation cost in the residential care can only partly covered by social assistance policy field. These two policy fields incompletely compensate with each other at this point.

Therefore, there are still gaps between the poverty threshold and the social assistance income support threshold, although other forms of basic security benefit include services, benefit payments and benefits in kind fill this gap to some extent. Moreover, empirical studies have indicated that there are more senior citizens entitled to social assistance benefit, but do not claim it due to feelings of shame or being afraid of financial loss for other family members, etc.

5.1.4 The interaction of ageing policy fields in the context of ageing policy

German pension policy field plays a main income source role for older people. It is the main factor that affects the ageing policy's living situation, but itself produces a high risk of hypothetical poverty risk in old age. Long-term care insurance plays an important role in supporting older people when they have to face physical and mental problems in Germany. It covers most parts of long-term care need under the new regulation and becomes even more comprehensive. These two policy fields interact with each on the basis of income and care needs. However, there are still gaps in between. Parts of the care costs can neither be covered by the long-term care insurance nor by pension benefits. And long-term care resources are only reachable under the detailed assessment procedure with a scoring system. Social assistance policy field plays a supplementary role in the German ageing policy. When long-term care insurance is not guaranteed to cover relatively limited long-term care needs, care assistance can be considered as another choice. However, care assistance level is not high enough. Only those older people included in care grades two to five can receive the benefits of the care assistance. What's more important is that social assistance policy field is designed to take into effect after the beneficiary's other resources are exhausted, which actually push those people especially old people close to theoretical poverty risk. Therefore, theoretically, the German old-age pension policy field, social assistance policy field and long-term care policy field cannot completely compensate for each other: neither of these policy fields can prevent poverty risk for older people totally by themselves, and the pension policy field has the main effect on older people's theoretical poverty risk condition, social assistance policy and long-term care policy field help to reduce poverty risk condition but still incompletely compensate with others.

5.1.5 Summary

In Germany, all fields of ageing policy are connected with poverty risks. Pension policy system produces relatively high poverty risks, particularly for women and widows. The basic benefit in the old age from German social assistance system can hardly improve this condition. The effectiveness of household-based pension to improve old age poverty risk is suboptimal for widows. Nevertheless, the size of the German pension depends on people's life course and how much they work during working age and job biography.

German long-term care policy, however, in principle produces fewer poverty risks for older people by its currently valid specific care grades and complex marking system with lower access threshold and its new care concept from 2017. Long-term care policy resources can better protect frail old people from poverty risks than before. But German has a long tradition of family care. Care responsibility and parts of care services still rely on care by family members, particularly women. The long-term care insurance pay contribution to the statutory pension pillar for care givers when they have to take care of one or more people in care grade two to five for at least 10 hours and at least two days a week at home while they are not employed for more than 30 hours a week. But in between, those family care givers whose care work does not reach this standard could suffer potential pension benefit lose, and parts of the family care givers have pushed to part-time job afterwards due to lasting of long-term care responsibility. The social assistance policy field eases theoretical poverty risks of older people only to some degree by basic benefit in the old age and coverage of accommodation cost in long-term care. However, since the older people have almost exhausted their living resources when they receive social assistance, they are highly exposed to theoretical poverty risks under these circumstances.

In the next part, I will discuss the poverty risk for older people of Denmark.

5.2 Poverty risk in old age in Denmark

This part discusses the poverty risks in Denmark by analyzing each policy field in the ageing policy package. By introducing policies' main features, access principles, policy benefits and generosity conditions, I analyse the interaction of ageing policies fields in the context of ageing policy.

5.2.1 Pension policy

5.2.1.1 Main features

The Danish pension policy is well marked by the three-pillar conceptual framework (Denmark country report, 2016). The main idea is that a fixed amount of money as a basic pension is guaranteed to every citizen regardless of the citizen's income and labour market participation situation over their whole career. The basic level of this pension is lower than in German. However, the guaranteed amount is very effective in protecting older people from poverty risk (Pfau-Effinger et al., 2011). The Danish pension system is "world class" even though with own drawbacks.

The first pillar of the Danish pension system is the public pension which is in the form of a universal basic pension with a means-tested supplement which has the impact that net gain from later retirement and extra pension savings or personal savings could be in a relatively low level. In the second pillar, labour market pensions are mandatory and can be adjusted or negotiated in the labour market with more than 12 per cent contribution rate for employees nowadays, and this rate has increased recently. The third pillar of Danish pensions consists of tax-subsidized pension arrangements, pension funds, individual saving schemes, banks and other forms of insurance company schemes. Tax-subsidized pension arrangements are tied until retirement and are offered by insurance companies. For many families, pension funds and other forms of the third pillar pensions are in the form of housing wealth (Denmark country report,2016).

5.2.1.2 Pension benefits

The universal public basic pension (Folkepension,earnings-tested) is about 838 Euros monthly paid per pensioner who must reside in Denmark for at least 40 years before reaching the normal retirement age. The Danish government pays contributions monthly or quarterly for this basic pension scheme. Besides this basic flat-rate pension, a means-tested supplement pension is paid as 448 Euros monthly married or cohabiting pensioners, and 904 Euros for single pensioners. (Statistic Denmark, 2018; European Statistic, 2018). The total amount of Danish basic public pension is 1,286 Euros for married or cohabiting pensioners and 1,742 Euros for single pensioners. In addition, a supplementary pension benefit (income-tested) is paid for old age pensioners as additional social benefits to help meet daily living and housing costs. The second pillar ATP (the Danish Labor Market Supplementary Pension) pension benefit is paid according to the insured's length of coverage as well as the number of contributions paid previously. ATP is collective insurance based, fully funded, statutory and defined-contribution scheme. It offers a lifelong pension for senior citizen reach the normal pension age. It also provides a "'survivors' lump sum benefit" for dependents. It has a wide coverage which includes almost all social security benefits, wage earners and the entire population. (SSPTW: Europe, 2016). The private and individual pension schemes are paid flexible based on voluntary agreements, while pension benefit from banks and insurance companies is based on the insurance model.

5.2.1.3 Access principles to pensions

The eligibility to reach Danish state pension is low, as long as citizens reach the pension age with 40 years of residency which actually cannot be considered as a precondition for Danish people, they can have the full state pension amount. But the basic public pension is earning-tested while basic supplement public pension is income-tested. The APP access for self-employment is voluntary.

5.2.1.4 Generosity level of pension policy field

The guaranteed minimum pension and the combination of this whole pension system help to strongly protect older people against low income. The total amount for Danish basic public pension is 1,286 Euros for married or cohabiting pensioners and 1,742 Euros for single pensioners, which are already high than Danish at-risk-of-poverty-threshold in 2017 as 12,729 Euros (1,060 Euros) for the single person (Statistic Denmark, 2018; European Statistic, 2018). Danish annual average income in 2017 is around 41,600 Euros (320,000 DKK) after tax (Statistic Denmark, 2018). Its net pension replacement rate is about 80.2 per cent which is higher than the average OECD figure as 63 per cent (OECD pension models, 2017). For those low earners, Danish net replacement rate is 110.3, ranks the highest level among OECD countries and much higher than the OECD average figure as 73 per cent. Due to Denmark has a comprehensive public basic pension scheme for senior citizens and comparably coherent pension system, the Danish pension policy field is generous and coherent, it protects older people from being exposed to poverty risk well. Of course, Danish pensioners need to pay tax on their income, but they are entitled to a tax-free annual personal allowance for the first 45,000 DKK, while the rest of their pension income is taxed at a rate of 41% to 55% (Statistic Denmark, 2017).

5.2.2 Long-term care policy

5.2.2.1 Main features

The Danish long-term care system is a universalistic system with the most extensive and decentralized long-term care resources in Europe. Unlike Germany, long-term care service in Denmark has historically been delivered as publicly financed service and organized as a care package (partly as home care and partly residential care) that is offered to all older people in need of care as a basic right stipulated by the Social Service Law. Care help for older people is the foremost responsibility and delivered by the state. Recipients do not have to be seriously ill, and care services are not offered regarding strict care grades or evaluating scores as Germany does.

5.2.2.2 Long-term care benefits

Danish home care is based on the public payment, and benefits are delivered in the form of personally and practical help which is organized in close collaboration with the recipient at home. Each municipality pays directly for service providers either private for-profit or non-profit public providers were chosen by recipients. But a for-profit provider must have certification by the municipality and includes services requested by the municipality. The municipality determines the content and scope of services and pays the same grants funds to services providers by the general level of service. Danish family care delivered by relatives has long been minimized, and family careers have already disappeared in Denmark. Instead, family members can be hired by the municipality as employees with public contracts and protection of their social security rights. Practically, Danes care about their old relatives more emotionally in the form of mental support and let actual care service be done by professional elderly services providers. For residential care, municipalities offer older people a temporary stay in a care centre or nursing home, or a longer stay in a special housing arrangement with free nursing attached (Danmarks Statistik, 2015a). Older people can choose institutions freely across municipal boundaries so that they can be close to their relatives and friends. In addition, since 1998, Denmark has provided at least two annual prophylactic visits to older people aged over 75 by a district nurse who evaluates their needs and helps them with better independent living (National Social Report from 2009 to 2014, Denmark). The purpose of this measure is to support senior citizens to have a better quality of life, and this preventive measure decreases forthcoming emergency care needs as well as postpones the real necessary care needs in reality. These preventive measures can evaluate and solve parts of potential health problems.

5.2.2.3 Access principles

Denmark long-term care access measures are comprehensive with universal approaches which have to compromise aspects of well-being. Eligibility for social care is decided by a special municipal service. There are no minimal requirements to entitle benefits from the local communities besides citizenship or the period that older people live in Denmark. The main principle of access is care needs including emotional and physical care needs. As long as older people have confirmation of care needs, they may entitle with comprehensive care services and benefits. Preventive care assessment has been done to older people even if they do not need care services yet.

5.2.2.4 Generosity level of long-term care policy field

In the ageing policy package of Denmark, long-care care resource is extensive and universal, and it widely covers different degrees of care needs without strict assessment. All long-term care resources are reachable by older people when they have needs. Denmark has a generous long-term care policy field. The state takes responsibility for long-term care practically, financially and responsibly.

5.2.3 Social assistance policy

The Danish social assistance policy field has been reformed after 2017, this system currently offers more individualized and flexibility solutions to people in different age groups (Denmark Report, 2017). Social assistance policy in Denmark for senior citizens with lower income is non-contributory, means-tested and non-taxed pension credit which covers reasonable, necessary expenses and medical expenses. Another form of support is "local welfare assistance" which is also considered as a kind of benefit of social assistance in local areas which support emergency financial payment.

The access principle of social assistance policy goes towards income and residency. Being at the low-income group and old is the key to access to this policy benefits. Local government has the authority to establish nursing homes and give aid to those with insufficient funds among older people.

Unlike other countries, social assistance policy in Denmark is generous and covers various aspects of living. This policy field covers the basic cost of living for older people and keeps them to live from being exposed to potential poverty risks. Therefore, measured regarding theoretical poverty this single policy field has a high degree of social protective possibility and helps to avoid the risk of poverty for older people.

5.2.4 The interaction of ageing policy fields in the context of ageing policy

Danish pension policy fields have effectively protected older people from suffering poverty risk by providing "well-diversified" three pillar pension policy, particularly for the fixed amount statutory basic pension and pension supplement. The combination of different pension schemes, older people has high degrees of income security. This system has created a safety policy environment protect against low-income for older people. With comparatively high pension replacement rate, Danish pension policy field ensures older people could have reasonable pension correlation to activities in the labour market. In the last year, the Danish pension system ranks first in the Melbourne Mercer Global Pension Index. The pension policy field itself has basically built circumstances for older people to be safe from potential poverty risk. Considering older people's long-term care needs, Denmark has a more favourable with less pressure and generous long-term care policy field, which fully covers long-term care needs for older people. In this point of view, the Danish long-term care policy field protects older people from being exposed to theoretical poverty risk by itself. In the combination of social assistance policy, Denmark has a high degree of social cohesion. Measured with potential poverty risk, Danish ageing policy is fairly egalitarian and does not leave gaps in hypothetical poverty risks for older people. On the contrary, it helps them to have a better quality of life, and each policy field compensates with each other for any shortfalls when older people have relatively difficulties. Ageing policy fields are generously interacted with each other and work well in avoiding senior citizens from theoretical poverty risk.

5.2.5 Summary

Poverty risks condition in old age in Denmark had been avoided by all ageing policy fields. One of the distinguishing characteristics of Denmark social welfare policy is that for most people who are not in the employment could access to forms of social transfer. However, there are also argues that these features have already created the low incentive for people to actively participate in the labour market. Besides comprehensive long-term care policy benefits, Danish family policy scores very well in the cross-national comparison. Family care for older people has also been covered by long-term care policy resources. One purpose is to allow women to participate in the labour market. Many of them return to work because of financial burdens while others for desires of having the career.

Notwithstanding, the Danish pension scheme has a high reputation in the international comparison, it has own problems. The basic public pension supplement in the first pension pillar is a means-tested scheme, which means the net gain for later retirement or from additional pension savings could be low. However, this problem does not have the necessary effect on poverty avoidance analysis. Nevertheless, Denmark pension policy field is rather complicated when shift analyzing point from avoiding potential poverty risk to higher benefit level. And should also be problems for citizens who are in so-called "residual pension group" (outside of compulsory "labor market pension"). These problems could be further analyzed in papers after this dissertation. In the next part, I will discuss the poverty risk for older people of the UK.

5.3 Poverty risk in old age in the UK

This part discusses the poverty risk in the UK by analyzing each policy field in the ageing policy package. Each policy field's main features, access principles, policy benefits and generosity levels are all included. Analysis of the interaction of ageing policy in the UK is also presented.

5.3.1 Pension policy

5.3.1.1 Main features

The UK has three tiers of old-age benefit system for older people. The first tier is the state pension. After the pension reform in 2016, the UK currently has a new state pension with a single tier. In the year 2018, the new state pension flat rate has been adjusted again. The UK first pillar pension has kept changing for several years, and its benefits have been increased.

The second tier is the old people's pension or over 80 pension which is a typical additional pension for senior citizens aged 80 and over (not based on national insurance contributions) (Government of United Kingdom Statistic system, 2016). The third tier is the attendance allowance which is a non-contributory, non-means tested pension scheme for disabled older people.

5.3.1.2 Pension benefits

The UK new full rate state pension is about 750 Euros per month (164.35 pounds per week) for a single person in 2018. The transitional rate below full rate is about 3 per cent, protected payment is about 3 per cent. The actual amount depends on the individual's national insurance record. The over 80 pension is about 334 Euros per month (73.30 pounds per week) minus the amount of any other state pension received. For example, if older people do not get the basic state pension or the new state pension or get less than 334 Euros per month, then they can get the pension gap paid up to 334 Euros per month (United Kingdom Public Sector Information, April 2016). Full benefit for the Attendance Allowance for disabled older people has two levels of rates. The higher level is paid about 390 Euros per month (£85.60 per week) while, the lower level is about 261 Euros per month (57.30 pounds per week) (the United Kingdom Public Sector Information, April 2016).

The UK government regulates that anyone over 65 pays tax if their total annual income adds up to more than their Personal Allowance of 18,240 Euros (16,000 pounds) per year. An annual income over 18,240 Euros (16,000 pounds) is taxed at various tax rates from 20% to 45% (UK government statistic, 2017). However, the first 25 per cent of the amount built up in any pension can be treated as a tax-free lump sum. Usually, a pensioner's basic income is much lower than the country's tax threshold (UK government statistic, 2017).

5.3.1.3 Access principles to pensions

Pension access principles in the UK are based on mean-tested and needs-tested schemes. Pensioners need at least ten qualifying years on their national insurance records to receive the new state pension. The full rate of single-tier pension is based on 35 qualifying years of national insurance credits or contributions. Pensioners aged 80 and over receive the over 80 pensions if they have been resident in the UK for at least ten years out of 20, and do not receive the state pension or the state pension is less than 73.30 pounds a week until now. The Attendance Allowance is a typically designed pension to help with extra costs when older people are disabled and in need of someone to take care of. Benefit recipients must over 65, reside in the UK for at least two of the last three years, and they must have been disabled (including g physical and mental disability, such as blindness and learning difficulties) for at least six months unless terminally ill. When older people get terminally ill, they can be automatically enrolled to get the higher rate Attendance Allowance once they are eligible.

5.3.1.4 Generosity level of pension policy field

Countries such as the UK have increased senior citizen's poverty risk by relying much more on commercial old age benefits and older people's initiative than state-run retirement pension schemes and funds (DWP, 2006). Nevertheless, the pension policy has already changed since 2016, the new state pension has replaced the old state pension, and the additional pension and this change probably makes the state pension almost universal. (details also shown in appendix1). But the limitation of this reform also concerns the time dimension. The new state pension has a certain start time, for women start from 6th of April, 1953 and for men starts from 6th of April, 1951, older people who were born before that year will have to continue entitled to the old state pension schemes. The old state pension benefit is even lower which includes a basic state pension about 574 Euros monthly (£73.30 per week) and an additional state pension which without a fixed amount (UK government statistic, 2017). This additional state pension is paid on the basis of how many year recipients paid national insurance and their earnings. Nevertheless, the old state pension benefit level is comparatively lower than the new state pension.

According to the UK Office for National Statistics, the UK whole economic average income is about 2,640 Euros monthly in 2018 (the UK Office for National Statistics, 2019). The net pension replacement rate by earnings for average earners is around only 29 per cent, which very much lower than the OECD average (63 per cent). For low earners, the UK net pension replacement rate is around 52 per cent, which is also lower than the OECD average level (73 per cent), only Poland (37 per cent) and Mexico (35 per cent) have lower replacement rate than the UK (OECD, 2018). The UK figures have been almost at the lowest level among OECD countries. Currently, older people have to theoretically face a high possibility of poverty. According to the UK statistics database, poverty level people age 75+ are about 18.5 per cent while the poverty levels of the whole population are 11 per cent (UK statistics, 2017). According to analysis in this dissertation, the at-risk-of-poverty threshold of the UK is around 1,049 Euros monthly in 2017, which is much higher than the UK new state pension as about 782 Euros per month (£ 168.6 per week) until now. Although with the introduction of the new singe-tier state pension (about 30 per cent higher than the old state pension), the income situation of older people is still serious. Besides, there is and going to be a long transition period. Currently, for those retirees who are unable to reach the new state pension will have no difference. Nevertheless, older people in the UK live under the poverty threshold, in the basic condition; even they have the new state pension. Private pension might help to fill this gap, but people have to have enough income during their working lives to make a contribution to the private pension insurance and buy their own homes. However, most older people who lack these resources will have to face poverty risk, and old women are the most affected group by old age poverty.

Family support in the UK is also very important and popular for older people, for example, widow's benefits. However, widow's benefits are at the mean level for the people over pension age. Only the Bereavement Payment which is paid as a lump sum of about 2,280 Euros (£ 2000) is eligible only when the dead partner or husband or wife was not entitled to a state pension. Therefore, the UK pension policy field cannot prevent older people been exposed to poverty risk, on the contrary, this policy system has caused the high possibility of potential old age poverty and must be prevented from rising.

5.3.2 Long-term care policy

5.3.2.1 Main features

The long-term care policy field in the UK is a means-tested system, and the level of benefit depends on people's capital, income and health conditions. It provides financial support and services to older people to cover basic long-term care needs. The long-term care assessment procedure is under a "targeted social rights, means-tested and needs-tested" model. Long-term care resources are reachable under comparatively strict assessment.

5.3.2.2 Access principles

To access care benefits, older people should meet certain criteria, and they are expected to pay for the full cost of care themselves including care home services if their assets are above a certain level. UK senior citizen sometimes needs to sell their homes to pay for long-term care costs, but long-term care services are heavily concentrated on older people aged over 85+ Low-income senior citizens in the UK can also claim a means-tested social assistance benefit as a non-taxed pension credit (UK Government Statistic, 2017) together with limited local welfare assistance. The access principles for long-term care policy in the UK are strict.

5.3.2.3 Long-term care benefits

Home care benefit in the UK is available to cover older people care costs only if their capital savings are between the lower threshold and the upper threshold. This is a weekly income, and the current rate is 1 pound for every 250 pounds between the lower and upper capital thresholds. Local authorities support senior citizens from about 50 pounds to different levels various across the UK. A care plan will be made, and a home care package will be delivered if care at home is appropriate by care recipients. The local authority may provide the services itself or employ private or voluntary organizations to provide care services. They can also make direct payments to individuals, so that these individuals can buy their own preferred care services if they have been assessed as needing help. The amount depends on the individual's needs, but it can only cover the necessary care costs, definitely not the whole picture.

Institutional care services are provided as care homes and nursing homes. Care homes are registered to provide personal care. They normally offer support and ensuring basic personal needs are taken care of. Nursing homes provide the same personal care as care homes do but also have an extra qualified nurse on duty 24 hours a day. However, long-term care benefit does not support accommodation costs which older people have to pay for themselves, and this part of the cost is huge and very expensive. Of course, housing costs are also excluded from long-term care policy benefits. Long-term care residential services are very expensive for care recipients and government. Usually, there are different care accommodation at different levels to meet different degrees of care requirements. Most residential care homes or nursing homes are run by independent sector, minorities are run by local authorities. In recent years, parts of local authorities have also subcontracted care homes to save costs.

In addition, like other countries, some kinds of care allowance benefits are available in the UK. Pensioners as couples can have income support as a personal allowance of 146 Euros (128.40 pounds) from the year 2017 to 2018. The UK carer's allowance is also available, but it is paid directly to carers who care for someone at least 35 hours a week as about 286 Euros (62.70 pounds) weekly, but not to care recipients.

5.3.2.4 Generosity level of long-term care policy field

If concerning long-term care policy resources itself in the

UK and comparing to care need for older people, this long-term care policy can only cover necessary care needs. Since analysis of long-term care policy assumes that long-term care policy itself covers the overall long-term care need of older people regardless of compensation of other policy fields, the UK long-term care policy field is unable to support older people from suffering hypothetical poverty risk by itself. Besides, not all parts of long-term care resources are reachable unless recipients pass the assessment procedure. When older people have to face high care costs and worse health condition, they have to sacrifice their saving and assets first until they are unable to afford. This policy field leaves gaps for older people for hypothetical poverty risk.

5.3.3 Social assistance policy

The social assistance policy field supports low-income older people in the UK with "pension credit" which can top up their income to about 804 Euros monthly (£176.4 weekly) by guarantee credit, about 743 Euros monthly (£163 per week), and saving credit, about 61 Euros monthly (13.4 pounds per week), for a single senior citizen. For couples whose income is below 726 Euros monthly (159.35 pounds weekly), the social assistance benefits can top up their income to about 1,134 Euros monthly (248.8 pounds per week) by guarantee credit, and by saving credit about 68 Euros monthly (14.99 pounds per week). But these schemes of social assistance benefits are a means-tested policy scheme with specific assessment criteria. Recipients must reside in the UK and reach pension credit qualifying age. For those older people who have severe disability, additional amount of pension credit is available: for single person is about 293 Euros monthly (64.30 pounds per week), and for couples are about 293 Euros monthly (64.30 pounds per week) (one the couples are qualified) and about 586 Euros monthly (128.60 pounds per week) (both couples are qualified). However, these benefits are not enough cover living costs by itself, and they are lower than the at-risk-of-poverty threshold. Besides, due to means-tested access principles of social assistance policy field, some groups of senior citizens are excluded from this part of the benefit. Therefore, the UK social assistance policy field cannot protect older people from being exposed to theoretical poverty risks. There are still gaps in between.

5.3.4 The interaction of ageing policy fields in the context of ageing policy

The UK pension policy field has typical liberal welfare states characteristic. Although a basic state new pension is provided as minimum pension, the benefit level is low. And the new state pension has a long transition period, current retirees might see no differences to change their living condition. Future retirees have to save more incomes to contribute the private pension scheme and buy themselves homes in order to improve their future old age poverty possibility, but if they are unable to obtain more income in the labour market, they might also have few resources after retirement.

Moreover, a large number of older people in the UK in bad health condition according to the OECD data. Among OECD countries, the UK disability of older people is more widespread than the other countries. About 20% of the over-80s are classified as obese in England in 2017. The obesity level among adults in the

UK has already doubled from 14% to 27% between 1990 and 2015 (OECD, 2017). The bad health condition of older people shows more pressure to the long-term care system. However, the UK long-term care policy field covers only necessary care needs not the whole picture, older people have to pay parts of care costs by themselves which many of them are unable to afford. Parts of long-term care resources are not easy to reach. Therefore, pension and long-term care policy field can only in part compensate each other. The social assistance policy field itself also cannot support older people live above the theoretical poverty threshold by itself. The UK social assistance benefits somehow contribute to decreasing theoretical old age poverty risk caused by pension system and long-term care system but far not enough. This policy scheme only partly compensates for long-term care policy filed.

5.3.5 Summary

Theoretical poverty risk in old age in the UK has been contributed by all fields of ageing policy. With the relatively lowest net pension replacement rate among OECD country, this pension policy field could make older people to be exposed to highly poverty risks. Different from sufficient Danish minimum state pension, the UK basic state pension level is very low, either for the new state pension or the old state pension with pension supplement. Besides having insufficient pension income, the UK older people also face bad health condition especially obesity which is an extremely common problem and one of the main risk factors causing old age health problem. Based on OECD data, more than 20 per cent of people aged 80+ are obese, but in other countries such as Denmark, this figure is less than 10 per cent (OECD, 2017).

Long-term care policy field in the UK cannot cover care needs well, this system leaves gaps between care needs and long-term care resources. The UK government is unable to compensate this gap as well because care needs such as residential accommodation cost are also expensive for the government. Many local authorities have subcontracted care homes to save costs. The effective option to solve this problem would be individuals have sufficient income by participating labour market and save more to pay for the private pension scheme and to buy themselves homes and pay for parts of care cost after retirement. However, minority retirees have accessed these resources. This situation is also reflected by the high poverty rate in the UK and income inequality condition. Therefore, pensions and long-term care policy fields incompletely compensate with each other, they leave gaps in between, and both cannot protect older people from being exposed to theoretical poverty risks. Unlike Denmark, the UK's social assistance system is weak, and does not play a role as the minimum guarantee policy.

In the next part, I will introduce a comparative perspective analysis on ageing policy and theoretical poverty risk, in which each empirical country's generosity condition of ageing policy as well as consequences for the poverty risk will be included.

5.4 Comparative perspective on ageing policy and poverty

5.4.1 Generosity conditions

5.4.1.1 Germany

The German ageing policy condition lies somewhere between

the UK and Denmark. With an insurance-oriented pension and improved long-term care systems, the criteria to access benefits for German ageing policy are loose than the UK but stricter than Denmark. The size of benefit is more generous than the UK, but less generous than Denmark. Pension income depends much more on contributions and personal funds. Its overall coverage of the pension insurance system can, to some extent, ensure older people have a basic standard of living. However, wide pension insurance coverage cannot guarantee basic income when the system does not include the basic or minimum pension. People who did not have full-time standard employment, whose labor market participation are interpreted such as by care responsibilities, or who were low-incomc earners even when they have full-time employment, are being exposed to poverty risk after retirement. Low income in the old age is more easily lead to bad health condition among older people.

Since 2017 Germany has lowered its long-term care benefits access threshold while comparatively increase long-term care benefits by providing new care concept and making care benefit more generous than before. Besides, this system further includes supports toward parts of daily care work, such as housework, and includes advisory consultant services for care recipients and family members in the long-term care insurance services, like Denmark does under the new regulation. However, one of very expensive care need items, the accommodation and food, are still excluded by long-term care benefit itself. Care related co-payment in residential care is still high, and it differs among care homes. These part of care costs incompletely covered by social assistance policy field based on the main principle that recipients are expected to reach social assistance benefits after their own resource are exhausted as we have discussed above. German social assistance policy field failed to provide overall basic protection for older people from being exposed to theoretical poverty risk. The basic retirement benefit offered by this system is far not enough to secure older people live above the at-risk-of-poverty threshold.

5.4.1.2 Denmark

From analyzing ageing policy generosity dimensions of Denmark in this dissertation, it can be seen that Denmark, on the one hand, has the least requirements for senior citizens to access to social benefits, on the other hand, it offers the most comprehensive basic pension as a fixed amount minimum pension which secures a comparatively higher income level and basic living. The basic Danish pension is around 838 Euros which are lower than the German average monthly pension. However, with a fixed mount basic pension supplement, the total amount could be around 1,286 Euros for married or cohabiting pensioners and around 1,742 Euros for single pensioners which are very effective in protecting older people from poverty risk. The generous Danish long-term care policy resource offers help to care recipients both physically and mentally. It comprehensively covers all long-term care needs, such as expenses, services and benefits. Older people do not have to wait until they are sick or being assessed whether they need assistance at certain grades or to meet fixed criteria to access services, and they do not need to pass the assessment procedures with either low or high thresholds.

Moreover, the social assistance policy scheme is also designed to cover the basic cost of living which fully protects older people with low income. Older people could access social assistance without exhausting their own resources. The Danish ageing policy is currently the most generous and nature comprehensive package among these three countries, and it protects older people well, which could be regarded as poverty more protected model.

5.4.1.3 The UK

In contrast, the UK has the most requirements to access benefits with the highest assessment entitlements for ageing policy. Although the UK offers a guaranteed minimum pension which is around 750 Euros monthly (in full amount) for older people by the new state pension, however, this minimum pension is lower than its at-risk-of-poverty threshold. Besides, many older people are unable to reach this full amount minimum pension because of not fulfilling entitlements. Concerning the low net pension replacement rate compares among the OECD countries and the UK pension policy design, older people are facing serious theoretical poverty risks after retirement. With low income and high old age poverty risk, older people have increased changes to suffer bad health. The actual data has also proved this point. However, when older people have the relatively high demand for care needs, the UK long-term care system failed to support them with incomprehensive long-term care resources. Assessment of recipients' assets and family financial conditions is one of the preconditions before recipients could access long-term care resources. If their assets are higher than the upper threshold, they must pay most of their long-term care costs themselves or rely on family support until they are unable to afford it. Besides, family care work in the UK is not popular compared with Germany. Care allowance is paid to careers directly not to care recipients as Germany does. Therefore, older people in the UK are in principle facing a higher risk of poverty risk than the other two countries. In addition, the UK social assistance policy field could have a positive effect to fill the gap. However, it is a means-tested policy scheme with specific and strong assessment criteria. Some older people are excluded from the UK social assistance system even though they need social support because they cannot pass this assessment procedure, and some are ashamed to claim for social support, or they do not want to embarrass or exhaust their relatives' resources since many social assistance assessment procedures contain family financial assessment. Therefore, the UK ageing policy is the least generous package, and older people are exposed to higher theoretical poverty risk, which could be regarded as poverty less protected model.

5.4.2 Consequences of theoretical poverty risk

5.4.2.1 Germany

In 2014, the at-risk-of-poverty threshold in Germany was set at 60 per cent of the median income of the entire population, below which 16.7 per cent of the population was found. German has a relatively high poverty rate of older people as 0.095 in comparison with other countries such as Denmark (0.032), France (0.033), Greece (0.082), Spain (0.054) and Austria (0.088) according to the OECD data. But German ranks lower than the UK as 0.131 concerning the old age poverty rate in the same year. However, German ranks low concerning the average pensions. In 2014, the net pension replacement rate was only 50 per cent in Germany which was lower than many other OECD countries such as Denmark, France, Greece, Spain and Austria except the UK which has only 29 per cent of replacement rate. In the year 2016, this replacement rate still stays at 51 per cent (OECD data,

2014,2016). In 2017, the net pension replacement rate is 51 per cent for average earner while 55 per cent for low earners. The net pension placement rate for low earner is about 18 per cent lower than the OECD average rate (OECD,2017). German at-risk-of-poverty threshold equals to monthly 1,060 Euros in 2017 (EU-SILC survey, Eurostat, 2018).

Since 2008 (below 15.2 per cent of the population), the proportion of the population at risk of relative poverty has steadily increased. But in the age group of 65 and over, or in the retirement phase, the risk of poverty is decreasing in both men and women, albeit to varying degrees in 2016 (Statistisches Bundesamt, 2016). Women were affected by a higher risk of poverty in almost all age groups than men, above average at 18.4 per cent at the poverty rate while men remained 14.0 percentages at this age group. And about 16.7% of the retired persons lived in households where the people were considered to be vulnerable to poverty (EU-SILC survey).

As a major old age income source, the amount of pension which is paid out depends on level and length of contribution under German insurance-oriented pension policy scheme. There is no basic fixed amount pension like Denmark does. No matter from which pension pillars older people receive their retirement income, they face a similar situation. Since the reform of 2001, manufacturing core workers can access occupational pension schemes at a batter chance, but this advantage cannot eliminate poverty risk for older people. This problem is caused by low pension contribution rate of the employers. In some pension schemes, for example, in the chemical industry, the pension contribution from the employees remains voluntary. Therefore, employer contribution stays at the minimum level, and no more contribution than that can be guaranteed (Ebbinghaus et al., 2010, p. 142). Other core workers, who are not entitled to pension schemes, rely on "Riester Pensions", which is based on a marketized commercial insurance system with a minor public subvention. With this pension scheme, there is no contribution part from the employers, and pension benefits rely totally on employees' voluntary contributions. Only 40 per cent of the eligible population has joined these pension plans, of whom a large proportion are higher-paid workers (Hagen and Kleinlein, 2012). Evidence shows that the "Riester Pensions" involves high and uncertain costs (Willert, 2011; Hagen and Kleinlein, 2012).

The basic security benefit which is offered by the German social assistance system supports senior citizens as a backup option. Senior citizens reach retirement age can claim basic security benefit if their income does not cover their basic need. By providing such as basic retirement benefit, the social assistance policy theoretically improves some older people's living condition but cannot protects them from the theoretical poverty risk since these benefits are at a very low level. There are still gaps between the poverty threshold and the social assistance benefits. Besides, empirical studies have indicated that older people are excluded from the social assistance benefit because of ashamed to claim. If the social assistance policy can only pay at the very low level, then it cannot completely compensate for the poverty risk which might be caused by pension policy. Therefore, hypothetically, the German old-age pension policy field and social assistance policy field cannot completely compensate for each other: neither of these two policy fields can prevent poverty risk for older people totally by themselves, and the pension policy field has the main effect on older people's theoretical poverty risk condition.

If considering long-term care policy field, we can see another picture. With the "Long-Term Care Insurance Act" (SGB Ⅺ) implemented in 1995/96, the German welfare state defines the responsibility for long-term care for older people as a task of the state. It is based on social insurance to which employees pay contributions, while all older people in need of care have the right to receive paid care, if they have been assessed by what a person can still do on their own and where they need assistance and support. All persons in need of long-term care have equal access to the benefits (Germany Federal Minister of Health, 2015).

The current long-term care policy resource is relatively generous. German home care payments range from 689 to 1,995 monthly from care grade two to care grade five. The size of residential care service covers old recipients in all care grades. The amount that is paid by care insurance differs according to the extent of each person's requirements. Full-time residential care service supports older people if they stay in residential households, i. e. a nursing home. A monthly lump sum from 125 (CG1) to 2,005 (CG5) has been guaranteed since 2016 (§ 45b SGB Ⅺ). Payments in 2016 were from 125 monthly to 901 range from care grade one to care grade five (§ 45b SGB Ⅺ). Then additional care benefit support is still available. Superficially, the long-term care policy scheme covers most care needed by older people including "hard cases", however, there are still gaps and the possibility that older people could suffer poverty risk. Co-payment in the residential care older people. And Germany long-term care has a high dependency on family care support.

Nevertheless, the federal government has increased family care givers' social security benefits by connecting long-term care policy field with the pension and unemployment insurance policy.

Family care givers will be paid for pension contributions by German long-term care insurance. These pension contributions will also rise if recipients' long-term care needs are increased. What should be mentioned is that family care givers can have 25 per cent extra pension contributions if they care for long-term care recipients under "hard cases" (CG5) whose care needs are extremely high. Moreover, the German federal ministry of health has claimed that the pension insurance may cover family care givers if they offer care work for relatives who suffer from serious conditions, for example, dementia, and in need of long-term care. Under the new regulation, free advisory care consultant both for care recipients and family members are available.

Besides, senior citizens who need long-term care but cannot receive enough services can receive support from the social assistance service, e. g. covering expenses in a home environment, assisting people with disabilities, providing long-term care or a cash payment for living expenses assistance. About one-third of all residents in German nursing homes receive social assistance. This means-tested social assistance system plays an essential role, particularly in this area. Due to the introduction of Germany's new long-term care bill and the second bill and relevant benefits improvement, the long-term care contribution rate has increased during 2017 by 0.2 per cent to 2.55 or 2.8 percentages points for childless persons. Therefore, the German long-term care policy field has widened its coverage and has been more comprehensive.

Each ageing policy field in Germany may cause poverty risk for older people and incompletely compensate with each other. The social assistance policy can only pay at the poverty level, therefore cannot completely compensate for poverty that is caused either by pension policies or long-term care policies or both. The poverty risk condition relies on the pension policy field in this country. Pensions as a main income source in German is a factor which affects the poverty risk condition for older people.

5.4.2.2 Denmark

In Denmark, the at-risk-of-poverty rate has stayed at the lowest level of all member states of the EU. The number of people who report being unable to feed themselves in Denmark is almost half of the EU-average (Society at A Glance, 2014). The poverty condition of Danish senior citizens is less serious than in most other countries, and so does its poverty risk for older people. Indeed, according to the Center for Global Development's Commitment to Development index, Denmark is at the first position in respect to overall commitment to social development and third place when it comes to reducing the burden of poverty. Denmark contributed 0.75 per cent of Gross National Income (GNI) to the UN target toward the development assistance in 2016 and contributed 0.85 per cent of GNI to the development aid in 2015. Although the new Danish liberal government has decided to reduce part of their development aid, the Danish contribution on this item is still higher than the UN recommendation (as 0.7 per cent of GNI) (Sustainable Governance Indicators, 2016).

Senior citizens are covered under both the universal old-age basic pension and pension supplement, which together comes to 1,286 Euros/1,742 Euros a month for married or cohabiting/a single person besides other additional benefit such as a deferral pension. A supplementary pension benefit is paid to pensioners to help meet daily living and housing costs. This basic pension package can fully exceed the poverty threshold (Statistic Denmark, 2017). Therefore, Denmark has a high level of pension benefits. Consequently, the Danish pension policy field can theoretically prevent poverty risk for older people by itself.

Unlike Germany, Denmark has a more service-oriented and comprehensive long-term care system that covers all citizens. Except for many specific cash benefit programs. Danish long-term care benefits are provided by services followed by specific functional help. Services must be provided and organized in close collaboration with the recipients in both home care and institutional care. Municipalities are responsible for ensuring that the individual receives the assistance that matches their needs and each municipality arranges for those who need institutional care.

Denmark has the most extensive and comprehensive long-term care policy for older people. Danish long-term care benefits are high, and services are largely available free of charge. Family care services offered by relatives has been minimized. Instead, they take care of their old relatives by emotional comfort. In Denmark, there are no more family care givers. Instead, family members are hired by municipalities as employees with public contracts. Their social security rights have been protected under employment regulations directly. Danish long-term care policy field not only focuses on older people's physical and mental needs like other countries, but also focuses more on preventive health protection (National Social Report from 2009 to 2014, Denmark). So, the long-term care policy field basically covers almost all care need senior citizens by itself (Statistic Denmark, 2013a, 2013i, 2014b), and the long-term care situation in Denmark is more favourable with less pressure and extremely generous than the other two countries. It can theoretically help to eliminate poverty risk for older Danish people.

Older people can also get help from the social assistance

policy scheme when they need it under rare situations, and there is no maximum duration for receiving the benefit. But benefits will be reduced after receiving assistance for six continuous months. For all age groups, the social system now offers more flexibility and individualized solutions (Sustainable Governance Indicators, 2016). "Local welfare assistance" is also considered as another benefit of social assistance in local areas which support emergency financial payment. Therefore, Denmark has a far more generous social assistance system which can theoretically ensure senior citizens live above the poverty threshold. All its ageing policy fields help to avoid poverty risk for older people in Denmark and its old age poverty risk condition is much better compared with the other two countries.

5.4.2.3 The UK

The population reporting that "they feel that they cannot afford to buy sufficient food" in the UK is higher (Society at A Glance, 2014) than the other two countries. Among all age groups in the UK, those over the age of 65 are at the greatest risk of theoretical poverty.

Senior citizens in the UK are currently covered by a new state pension as a basic pension and the over 80 pensions and the Attendance Allowance. The full new state pension is less than the at-risk-of-poverty threshold, and this old age pension has limitations. Besides, many older people are still stuck by the old state pension scheme whose benefit level is even lower because of the policy transition period. Although the UK guaranteed minimum pension supports older people with basic living costs, there are big gaps between the poverty threshold and pension income, which lead to senior citizens theoretically being exposed to poverty risk. Other tiers of pension benefit are available for senior citizens to fill this gap and they may have multiple choice such as private pension schemes, but all other pension choices are only available according to the individual's financial situation and contributions. Therefore, theoretically, the UK pension policy field does not prevent older people from being exposed to poverty risk by itself.

When considering the social assistance policy field, it supports low-income senior citizens in the UK with "pension credit", but this income level is still lower than the poverty threshold. Moreover, it is a means-tested policy scheme with specific assessment criteria. As a result, some senior citizens are even excluded from this type of benefit. Therefore, instead of eliminating poverty risk, social assistance policy in the UK also theoretically leaves more gaps to poverty risk for older people.

When concerning the UK's long-term care benefit provision, we get a new picture. On the one hand, whether older people could reach long-term care resources depends on people's capital savings. Each local authority will support senior citizens if their savings are between the lower threshold and the upper threshold. People with savings below the lower threshold will receive funding from social services. Some senior citizens are excluded from care costs support due to this capital saving assessment measure.

On the other hand, home care benefit is only available for senior citizens followed by care assessment. Although nursing homes in the UK can also support older people directly such as personal care and 24 hours carrying nursing tasks, however, the major care costs item such as accommodation is excluded. Hence, these policy benefit is still far not enough to protect older people from hypothetical poverty risk.

To some extent, pension benefits in the UK can cover some

of the living costs of older people, but it still leaves gaps to the theoretical poverty risk by itself. The UK long-term care policy field can eliminate parts of poverty risk, but not the whole picture. Therefore, each ageing policy field itself does not prevent poverty risk for older people by themselves in this country.

To summarize, a theoretical typology of three empirical countries of their ageing policy's impact in preventing poverty risk for older people can be explained (Table 1).

5.4.3 Summary

The main assumption of this dissertation is that ageing policy differs in their impacts on avoiding poverty risk for older people in European welfare states for senior citizens. With regarding this assumption, the findings have supported it. Different policy fields in the ageing policy package in different countries have their own effect on the degrees of preventing older people's hypothetical poverty risk. Countries like Denmark can fully protect senior citizens from old age poverty risk by ageing policy, countries like German and the UK expose their senior citizens to poverty risk at different levels. But Germany fixes this poverty risk by its long-term care policy field to some degrees, and the UK partly fixes this poverty risk mostly by its basic new state pension benefits.

Chapter 6 Conclusion

The main research question of this dissertation is how ageing policy differ in their hypothetical impact on poverty risk of older people in European welfare states.

A theoretical approach of "ageing policy" is introduced in this dissertation. This approach is based on the interaction of three policy fields in the ways in which they are framing social inequality and poverty of older people. Besides policies regarding pension and long-term care, it also includes social assistance policy. It is argued that all three types of policies are highly relevant in their role with regard to the risk of poverty in old age. In addition, I also introduce an "ideal-typical" typology of different types of ageing policy that are based on different ways in which ageing policy hypothetically impact on poverty risk for older people. Based on this theoretical framework, I develop the main hypotheses of the study, according to which differences between welfare regimes according to Esping-Andersen (1990) contribute to the explanation of differences between ageing policies and related poverty risks.

The interaction of ageing policy is analyzed by their generosity and the hypothetical impact on preventing poverty risk for older people.

The empirical study compares ageing policies and the connected poverty risks in three welfare states, Germany, Denmark and UK which differ with regard to the type of welfare regime which they present. They are measured at the level of institutional regulation itself. It measures the degree of generosity of each single policy field and of the whole fields of ageing policy together, and the related poverty risks. Two dimensions are used to measure generosity levels of ageing policy, the eligibility requirements before an individual has access to social benefits and the size of benefits.

The findings support the assumption regarding the role of differences between welfare regimes for the explanation of cross-national differences in ageing policies and related poverty risks for older people.

Germany represents the conservative welfare regime with "poverty medium protected model". In its ageing policy all ageing policy fields contribute to the poverty risks for older people and incompletely compensate with each other. Denmark represents the social democratic welfare regime with a "poverty more protected model". In its ageing policy, all policy fields help to avoid poverty risk for older people. And the UK represents the liberal welfare regime with a "poverty less protected model". In its ageing policy, not all policy fields help to avoid poverty risk for older people and they also do not compensate each other".

For more details, by analyzing the integration of three policy fields of ageing policy, Germany ageing policy's generosity condition is at the medium level in all dimensions. The German ageing policy is highly insurance-oriented and older people's income is strongly related to length and levels of working contribution. For older people who did not have lifelong full-time employment, they might suffer substantial risk of old age poverty from the pension system. To some degree, this gap can be compensated by the basic retirement benefit from social assistance policy field. However, this benefit is at the minimum level. There is no big difference when older people are exposed to potential poverty risk with this benefit. Therefore, it does not help to avoid hypothetical poverty risk. There is also another gap concerns to German long-term care system. The newly introduced long-term care bills have further strengthened long-term care benefits and show new care concept. It is more generous now after the reform of 2016 which has been well integrated into the German ageing policy even with unavoidable drawbacks. However, it still cannot completely fill gaps and prevent older people from hypothetical poverty risk. All ageing policy fields in Germany may contribute to the poverty risk for older people and incompletely compensate with each other. Pension as a main income source for senior citizens in this country is a main factor in affecting how serious the hypothetical poverty risk condition can become for older people. But pension policy field itself makes a relatively high share of contribution to poverty risk for older people by being short of basic pension or minimum pension. These results are coherent with the real data analysis, for example, in the report of "Entwicklung der Altersarmut bis 2036" ("Development of old age poverty until 2036") developed by German Institute for Economic Research and Center for European Economic Research last year, reflects poverty conclusion and poverty development of older people in Germany. It shows the risk of poverty increases overtime in Germany and the overall old-age poverty rate is only slightly reduced by the pension reform proposals under consideration (Haan et al., 2017).

Denmark has far more generous ageing policy compared with the other two countries in all dimensions with the relatively low level of hypothetical poverty risk for older people. All of its ageing policy fields help to prevent theoretical poverty risk by themselves as well as completely compensate with each other. With the comparatively comprehensive long-term care policy field and generous social assistance policy field and “world-class” pension system, the Danish ageing policies can eliminate poverty risk for older people. The Danish social assistance policy field also has a preventative impact on older people suffering the poverty risk at a basic level. Nevertheless, Denmark ageing policy is not “perfect”. This overall ageing policy could or might strongly decrease people’s incentives to save for retirement.

The UK has the least generous ageing policy in all respects, with a relatively high level of poverty risk for older people. Each ageing policy field itself does not prevent theoretical poverty risk. The big problem comes from pension policy field due to the low net pension replacement rate and low minimum pension. The UK long-term care policy field can only partly protect older people from poverty risk. It does offer benefits and services to satisfy long-term care needs, but these are not sufficiently generous. Pensions and long-term care policy can incompletely compensate with each other, but they leave gaps which contribute to exposed older people to theoretical poverty risk. Unlike Denmark, the UK’s social assistance does not play a role as the basic guarantee policy.

Therefore, ageing policies differ in their impacts on avoiding hypothetical poverty risk for older people in three different European welfare states. This difference is due to the design of each country’s ageing policy. Pensions, as the main income source for older people play a basic role in preventing them from this poverty risk or make contributions to old age poverty risk. When the guaranteed basic minimum pension was set and paid at a higher level, older people can receive adequate basic protection, such as in Denmark, which hypothetically prevents older people from poverty risk. However, other countries such as the UK which also have a basic minimum pension but at a much lower level cannot avoid poverty risk and have very low net pension replacement rate. Although older people are covered by the social assistance policy in some cases, it is still hard to say that these people do not suffer the hypothetical poverty risk. In country like German in which minimum pension is means-tested, low benefit level with restricted benefit period, older people could suffer high risk of poverty.

In the long run, my research also shows that there is a trend that old age theoretical poverty risks in Germany will be extended in the future, which is also announced in Entwicklung der Altersarmut bis 2036": the risk of old-age poverty in Eastern German will rise sharply over time, by 2031—2036, the old-age poverty risk for East Germany will nearly double compared to the risk in West Germany, and the poverty rate will increase to about 36% (Haan et al., 2017). And the UK ageing policy will contribute to extremely high contribution to theoretical old age poverty risk if the UK pension policy field cannot be improved in the first place of pension replacement rate.

Altogether, this dissertation can make an innovative contribution to comparative welfare state research and analysis of poverty in old age. It offers a new typology for comparative analysis about the role of welfare state policies for poverty of senior citizens that takes into consideration that poverty risks of people in old age should be understood as the result of the interplay between different types of welfare state policies.

However, in reality, the risk of poverty for older people is related to a much wider range of life in reality such as health, life expectancy, literacy ability, etc., the definition of poverty risk for older people mentioned in this dissertation is merely a minor aspect. Poverty can also be considered as an aggregation of drawbacks, the worry about self-vulnerability and the concern about many types of living risks, and lack of worthy rights and voice in daily lives.

In the future, more research analysis in this field is needed, and further questions should be analyzed. Poverty definitions as well as poverty types and poverty risk have widened broadly. For example, more policy fields should be included such as health policy and housing policy which may also have an influential effect on the poverty risk of older people in policy integration research. Along with long-term care reforms in many European welfare states, long-term care policy and poverty should have further and deeper interrelationship. It would be important to analyzc what level do European welfare states help to avoid poverty risk of older people: a hypothetical policy evaluation research towards long-term care. However, since this dissertation introduces a complex explanatory framework and a new method for its analysis, these two types of policies are not included yet. This is also the limitation of my findings on the basis of my methodological approach, and I hope to include more welfare states and more welfare policy fields in the future.

Finally, it must be emphasized that this dissertation is mainly focused on ageing policy fields and poverty risk for older people, but it does not mean that ageing policies only contribute to poverty risk for older people or only avoid poverty. Ageing policies have made great contributions to the social and economic development and increase living conditions and life quality for senior citizens, which have already shown us an open window of opportunity in human development. These policy fields will be changed and developed in coming decades which will become valuable references for later generations and an important part of social history.

Reference

Adena, M. and Myck, M. (2013). Poverty and Transitions in Health. *DIW* Berlin Discussion Paper No. 1319. Available at SSRN: https://ssm.com/abstract=2327439 or http://dx.doi.org/10.2139/ssm.2327439

Ahonen, P. (2011). *Strategy in the Public: Mediation of Strategy in Public Debate*. Paper presented at the Critical Management Studies Conference 2011. Naples, 11-13 July 2011.

Alkire, S. and Foster, J. (2011). Counting and Multidimensional Poverty Measurement. *Journal of Public Economic*, Vol. 95, now 7-8: 476-87.

Alkire, S. and Santos, M. E. (2010). *Acute Multidimensional Poverty: A New Index for Developing Countries*. United Nations Development Programme Human Development Report Office Background Paper No. 2010/11. P. 7.

Alkire, S. and Santos, M. (2014). Measuring Acute Poverty in the Developing World: Robustness and Scope of the Multidimensional Poverty Index. *World Development*, Vol. 59: 251-74.

Alkire, S., Foster, J., Santos, M., Seth, S., Ballon, P. and Roche, J. (2015). *Multidimensional Poverty Measurement and Analysis*. Oxford: Oxford University Press.

Andrews, E. S., Wang, D. K., Rofmann, R., Palmer, Fornero, E., Ferraresi, P. M., Jorge, S. M., Valdes-Prieto, S., Piggott, J.

and Bateman, H. (2006). *Pension Reform and the Development of Pension Systems: An Evaluation of World Bank Assistance*, Vol. 1.

Arts, W. and Gelissen, J. (2002). Three world of welfare capitalism or more? A state of the art report. *Journal of European Social Policy*, 12: 137.

Arza, C. and Kohli, M. (2008). *Pension reform in Europe: Politics, policies and outcomes*. London: Routledge.

Atkinson, B. A. (2015). *Inequality What Can Be Done?* Massachusetts London, England: Harvard University Press Cambridge.

Atkinson, T., Cantillon, B., Marlier, E. and Nolan, B. (2002). *Social Indicators: The EU and Social Inclusion*. Oxford: Oxford University Press.

Aurich, P., Frericks, P., Och, R. and Pfau-Effinger, B. (2014). *Local Welfare System Supporting Female Employment in Hamburg*. FLOWS working paper No. 31.

Babajanian, B. and Hagen-Zanker, J. (2012). *Social Protection and Social Exclusion: An Analytical Framework to Assess the Links*, ODI Background Note, London: Overseas Development Institute.

Böckman, O. (2011). Escaping Welfare? Social Assistance Dynamics in Sweden. *Journal of European Social Policy*, Vol. 21(5): 494-500.

Bambra, C. (2004). The world of welfare: illusory and gender blind. *Social Policy and Society*, *Vol*. 3, *Issue* 3: 201-211.

Barrientos, A. (2006). *Ageing, Poverty, and Public Policy in Developing Countries: New Survey Evidence*. Sigtuna, Sweden: Paper at the FISS 13th International Research Seminar on Issues in Social Security 'Social Protection in an Ageing World'.

Basu, K. and Stiglitz, J. E. (2016). *Inequality and Growth: Patterns and Policy, Volume I: Concepts and Analysis*. UK: Palgrave Macmillan UK.

Bjöklund, A. and Freeman R. B. (1997). Generating Equality and Eliminating Poverty—The Swedish Way. *The Welfare State in Transition: Reforming the Swedish Model*, edited by Freeman, R. B., Topel, R. and Swedenborg, B. Chicago: University of Chicago Press.

Blank, R. M. (2008). Presidential Address: How to improve poverty measurement in the United States. *Journal of Policy Analysis & Management*, 27(2): 233-254.

Blank, R. M. and Card, D. (2008). The Changing Incidence and Severity of Poverty Spells Among Single Mothers. *American Economic Review*, 98(2): 389-391.

Blank, R. M. and Greenberg, M. H. (2008). *Improving the Measurement of Poverty*. (The Hamilton Project Discussion Paper No. 2008-17). Washington, D. C.: The Brookings Institution.

Bönke, T. (2010). *Essays on Income Inequality, Poverty and Mobility*. Doctoral Dissertation. Berlin: Wirtschaftswissenschaft des Fachbereichs Wirtschaftswissenschaft der Freien Universität Berlin.

Börsch-Supan, A. and Quinn, C. (2015). *Taxing Pensions and Retirement Benefits in Germany*. Munich, Germany: Presented paper on CEPAR and CESifo workshop.

Bonoli, G. (2003). Two Worlds of Pension Reform in Western Europe. *Comparative Politics*, Vol. 35, No. 4 (Jul., 2003): 399-416.

Booth, C. (1903). *Life and Labour of the People of London. Second Series, Industry*, Vol. 5. London: Macmillan & Co.

Borchost, A. (1994), Welfare state regimes, women's interests and the EC, in Sainsbury, D. (ed.). *Gendering Welfare States*. London: Sage.

Bourguignon, F. and Fields, G. (1990). Poverty Measures and Anti-Poverty Policy. *Recherches Economque de Louvain*, Vol. 56, now 3-4: 409-27.

Brady, D. (2003). The Politics of Poverty: Left Political Institutions, the Welfare State, and Poverty. *Social Forces*. The University of North Carolina Press.

Brady, D. (2005). The welfare state and relative poverty in rich Western democracies. 1967—1997. *Social Forces*, 83: 1329-1364.

Brady, D. (2009). *Rich Democracies, Poor People: How Politics Explain Poverty*. Oxford: Oxford University Press.

Brady, D. and Burton, L. M. (2016). *The Oxford Handbook of the Social Science of Poverty*. New York: Oxford University Press.

Brady, D., Fullerton, A. S., and Cross, J. M. (2010). More Than Just Nickels and Dimes: A Cross-National Analysis of Working Poverty in Affluent Democracies. *Social Problems*, 57(4): 559-85.

Bridgen, P. and Meyer, T. (2014). The liberalisation of the German social model: public-private pension reform in Germany since 2001. *Journal of Social Policy*, 43 (1): 37-68.

Bridger, S. and Pine, F. (1998). *Surviving Post-socialism: Local Strategies and Regional Responses in Eastern Europe and The Former Soviet Union*. London: Routledge.

Brückner, H. and Mayer, K. U. (2005). De-standardization of the life course: What it might mean? And if it means anything, whether it actually took place? *Advances in Life Course Research*, 9: 27-53. doi: 10. 1016/S1040-2608(04)09002-1.

Budowski, M. and Tillmann, R. (2006). *Pauvreté et exclusion sociale en Suisse*. In Fundación Debate. Conference: Estado de bienestar en España y Suiza. Aspectos económicosy sociales, June 16-18, Bern.

Burtless, G. and Smeeding, T. M. (2001). *The Level, Trend and Composition of Poverty: Understanding Poverty*. New York Cambridge, MA: Russell Sage Foundation and Harvard University Press.

Bussemaker, J. and Kersbergen, K. (1994). Gender and the welfare state: some theoretical reflections. in D. Sainsbury (ed.). *Gendering Welfare States*. London: Sage.

Byrne, D. (2005). *Social Exclusion*. Open University Press. NewYork, USA. ISSN/ISBN: 0335215947.

Caldwell, M. (2004). *Not by Bread Alone. Social Support in the New Russia*. Berkeley: University of California Press.

Callan, T., Nolan, B., Walsh, J. R., Whelan, C. T. and Maitre, B. (2008). *Tackling Low Income and Deprivation: Developing Effective Policies*. Dublin: ESRI.

Campbell, J. R. and Holland, J. (2005). Development Research: Convergent or Divergent Approaches and Understandings of Poverty? An Introduction. *Focaal: European Journal of Social Anthropology*, 45: 3-17.

Carilin, G. and Gerhard, I. (2009). Long-term Care in Germany and the UK. *Social Policy in Aging Societies*, 9: 202-231.

Carlo, C. (2011). *The Challenge of Public Pension Reform in Advanced and Emerging Economies*. Prepared by the Fiscal Affairs Department. International Monetary Fund.

Carrera, L., Redwood, D. and Adams, J. (2011). *The Implications of Government Policy for Future Levels of Pensioner Poverty*. Pensions Policy Institute. London, UK. ISBN 978-1-906284-19-0.

Castleman T., Foster, J. E. and Smith C. S. (2015). Chapter 3, Person Equivalent Headcount Measures of Poverty. *Inequality and Growth Patterns and Policy. Volume I: Concept and Analysis*. Springer Nature. Palgrave macmillan, London.

Castleman, T., Foster, J. E. and Smith, C. S. (2016). Person Equivalent Headcount Measures of Poverty. In Basu, K. and Stiglitz, J. E. (eds). *Inequality and Growth: Patterns and Policy*. Palsgrave Macmillam, New York, USA.

Castles, F. G. (1998). *Comparative Public Policy: Pattern of Post-war Transformation*. Cheltenham: Edward Elgar.

Castles, F. G. and Mitchell, D. (1993). Worlds of Welfare and Families of Nations. In Castles, F. G (ed.). *Families of Nations: Patterns of Public Policy in Western Democracies*. Aldershot: Dartmouth Publishing Company.

Chakravarty, S. R. (2009). *Inequality, Polarization and Poverty*. New York: Springer-Verlag New York.

Chen, S. and Ravallion, M. (2001). How Did the World's Poor fare in the 1990s? *Review of Income and Wealth*, Vol. 47 (3): 283-300.

Chen, S. and Ravallion, M. (2010). The Developing World is Poorer than We Thought, but No Less Successful in the Fright against Poverty. *Quarterly Journal of Economics* 125: 1577-1625.

Chen, S. and Ravallion, M. (2012). *Absolute Poverty Measures for the Developing World. Chapter* 20 *in Measuring the Real Size of the World Economy*. Washington, DC: World Bank.

Chen, S. and Ravallion, M. (2013). More Relatively Poor People in a Less Absolutely Poor World. *Review of Income and Wealth*, 59: 1-28.

Chou, Y. and Kröger, T. (2014). Reconciliation of Work and Care among Lone Mothers of Adults with Intellectual Disabilities: The Role and Limits of Care Capital. *Health and Social Care in the Community*, 22 (4): 439-448.

Chou, Y., Pu, C., Kröger, T. and Fu, L. (2010). Caring, Employment and Quality of Life: Comparison of Employed and Nonemployed Mothers of Adults with Intellectual Disability. *American Journal on Intellectual and Developmental Disabilities*, 115 (5): 406-420.

Chou, Y., Tzou, P., Kröger, T. and Lee, W. (2008). Respite Care as a Community Care Service: Factors Associated with the Effects on Family Carers of Adults with Intellectual Disability in Taiwan. *Journal of Intellectual & Developmental Disability*, 33 (1): 12-21.

Cimadamore, K., Koehler, G. and Pogge, T. (2016). *Poverty and the Millennium Development Goals: A Critical Look Forward*. London: Zed Books.

Clarke, S. (2002). *Making Ends Meet in Contemporary Russia. Secondary Employment, Subsidiary Agriculture and Social Networks*. Cheltenham, UK: Edward Elgar.

Coromaldi, M. and Zoli, M. (2012). Deriving Multidimensional Poverty Indicators: Methodological Issues and An Empirical Analysis for Italy. *Social Indicators Research*, 107(1): 37-54.

Costanzo, Ranci, C. and Pavolini, E. (2015). Not all That Glitters is Gold: Long-term Care Reforms in The Last Two Decades in Europe. *Journal of European Sociology*, Vol. 25(3): 270-285.

Cousins, M. (2007). *Welfare Policy and Poverty*. Dublin: Institute of Public Administration.

Daly, M. (1994). Comparing welfare states: towards a gender

friendly approach. in Sainsbury, D. (ed.). *Gendering Welfare States*. London: Sage.

DeNavas-Walt, C., Carmen, Proctor, B. D. and Smith, J. C. (2012). *Income, Poverty, and Health Insurance*: 2011-*Current Population Reports*. U. S. Census Bureau.

Deutsche Rentenversicherung. (2010). *Versicherte und Rentner: Informationen zum Steuerrecht*. Berlin: Deutsche Rentenversicherung, 5. Edition (9/2010), 105.

Dewilde, C. (2003). A life-course perspective on social exclusion and poverty. *The British Journal of Sociology*, *Volume* 54, *Issue* 1, 109-128. DOI: 10.1080/0007131032000045923.

Diener, E., Oishi, S. and Lucas, R. (2002). Subjective Well-Being. The Science of Happiness and Life Satisfaction. *Handbook of positive psychology*. Oxford: Oxford University Press.

Directorate-General for Employment, Social Affairs and Inclusion of the European Commission and the Social Protection Committee. (2012). *Pension adequacy in the European Union*, 2010—2050. *Publications Office of the European Union*, Luxembourg, ISBN 978-92-79-25951-7.

Döhner, H. and Rothgang, H. (2006). Pflegebedürftigkeit. Zur Bedeutung der Familien Pflege für die Sicherung der Langzeitpflege. *Bundesgesundheitsblatt-Gesundheitsforschung-Gesundheitsschutz*, (6), 583-594.

Doetter. F. L. and Schmid A. (2018). Share Housing Arrangements in Germany-An Equitable Alternative to Long Term Care Services beyond Homes and Institutions. *International Journal of Environmental Research and Public Health*, 2018, 15: 342.

Dotter, C. (2015). *Essays on Poverty Measurement and Trade*. Universität Göttingen, Regensburg, Germany: Unpublished doctoral dissertation.

Dotter,C.(2017). *Can the World Bank's International Poverty Line reflect extreme poverty*? Courant Research Centre: Poverty,Equity and Growth-Discussion Papers,No.232: 3-4.

Dotter,C. and Klasen,S.(2014a). *The Concept of Relative Multidimensional Poverty: An Illustration using Indian DHS data*. Paper presented at the 33rd Annual Conference of the IARIW,Rotterdam,2014.

Dotter,C. and Klasen,S.(2014b). *The Multidimensional Poverty Index: Achievements, Conceptual and Empirical Issues*. UNDP Occasional Papers.

Dowd, R.(2013). A critical evaluation of Esping-Andersen's The Three Worlds of Welfare Capitalism. *Regent's Partk Social Policy Tutorial*. Micharlmas.

Duclos,J. Y.,and Araar,A.(2006). *Poverty and Equity: Measurement, Policy and Estimation with DAD*. New York: Springer.

Ebbinghaus,B.(2016). *Ageing Europe's Invisible Plight: Rising Income Inequality in Old Age Due to Employment Flexibilization and Pension Marketization*. Unpublished working paper presented on SASE Conference,University of California,Berkeley,June 24th to June 26th,2016.

Ebbinghaus,B., Gronwald, M. and Wiβ, T.(2010). Departing from Bismarckian public pension,in B. Ebbinghaus (ed.). *The Various of Pension Governance: Pension Privatization in Europe*. Oxford:Oxford University Press.

Ebbinghaus,B., Hofäcker, D.(2013). Reversing Early Retirement in Advanced Welfare Economies A Paradigm Shift to Overcome Push and Pull Factors. *Comparative Population*

Studies-Zeitschrift für Bevölkerungswissenschaft Vol.38,4 (2013):807-840.

Eichler,M. and Pfau-Effinger,B.(2009).The "consumer principle" in the care of elderly people-free choice and actual choice in the German welfare state. *Social Policy and Administration*,43,6:617-633.

Emmerson,C. and Muriel, A.(2008). Financial resources and well-being. In Banks, J., Breeze, E., Lessof, C. and Nazroo,J.(eds). *Living in the 21st Century: Older People in England*. The 2006 English Longitudinal Study of Ageing, Wave 3:118-149. London: Institute for Fiscal Studies.

Ervik R. and Lindén,T. S.(2013). The Making of Ageing policy, Theory and Practice in Europe. *Social Policy & Administration*. ISBN 978-1-78195-247-4.

Esping-Andersen,G.(1990). *The three world of welfare capitalism*. Cambridge: Polity Press.

European Commission.(2011). *Annual Review on Employment and Social Developments in Europe*. Commission staff working paper,Chapter 3,Brussels.

European Commission.(2014). Employment (main characteristic and rates)-annual average [lfsi_emp_a], Last updated: 08-10-2015.

European Union.(2016).Council of the European Union: Joint Report on Health Care and Long-term Care Systems and Fiscal Sustainability. Oct. Issue.

European Union.(2016).Council of the European Union: Social Protection Performance Monitor (SPPM)-Report.

Falcon,J.(2012). Temporal trends in intergenerational social mobility in Switzerland: A cohort study of men and women born between 1912 and 1974. *Swiss Journal of Sociology*,

38,153-175.

Feargel,M.(2018).Poverty in the UK:statistics. *House of Commons Library*,02(20),No.7096.

Federal Ministry of Health.(2017).Pflegeleistungen nach Einführung des 1.Pflegestärkungsgesetz es,Germany.

Federal Ministry of Health.(2017).Peer Review on "Germany's Latest Reforms of the Long-term Care System",Long-term Care in Germany.

Federal Statistical Office.(2016). *Older People in Germany and the EU*. Wiesbaden:Federal Statistical Office.

Ferreira,F.H.G.and Maria A.Lugo.(2013).Multidimensional Poverty Analysis:Looking for a Middle Ground. *The World Bank Research Oberserver*,IKSO13.

Ferreira,F.H.G.and Ravallion,M.(2009).Poverty and Inequality:The Global Context. In Salverda,W.,Nolan,B. and Smeeding,T.(eds.). *The Oxford Handbook of Economic Inequality*. Oxford:Oxford University Press.

Ferreira,F.H.G.and Ravallion,M.(2011).Poverty and Inequality: The Global Context: 599-638. *The Oxford Handbook of Economic inequality*, edited by Salverda, W., Nolan, B. and Smeeding,T.M.Oxford:Oxford University Press.

Ferreira,F.H.G.,Chen,S.,Dabalen,A.,Jolliffe,D.,Narayan, A.,Prydz,E.B.,Revenga,A.P.,Sangraula,P.and Dikhanov,Y.(2015). *A Global Count of the Extreme Poor in 2012:Data Issues,Methodology and Initial Results*. Manuscript. Washington,DC:The World Bank.

Firlit,E.and Chlopecki,J.(1992).When Theft is Not Theft. In *The Unplanned Society:Poland during and after Communism*.ed.J.Wedel:95-109.New York:Columbia University Press.

Fritzell, J., Ritakallio. V. M. (2010). Societal Shifts and Changed Patterns of Poverty. *International Journal of Social Welfare*, 19 (s1): S25-S41, April.

Foster, L. (2011). Older people, pensions and poverty: An issue for social workers? *International Social Work*, Vol. 54, No. 3: 344-360.

Gabriele, K. (2016). *Looking back and Looking forward: The Case for A Developmental Welfare State*. Poverty and The Millennium Development Goals. The University of Chicago Press, USA.

Gabriel, R. (2015). *Inequalities within progress. Social stratification and the life course among older people population in Switzerland* 1979—2011 (*Unpublished doctoral dissertation*). University of Geneva.

Gans, J. H. (1972). The Positive Functions of Poverty. *American Journal of Sociology*, Vol. 78, No. 2 (Sep., 1972): 275-289.

Gasior, K., Huber, M., Lamura, G., Lelkes, O., Bernd, M., Rodrigues, R., Schmidt, A., Zólyomi, E. (2012). *Facts and Figures on Healthy Ageing and Long-term Care: Europe and North America*. European Centre for Social Welfare Policy and Research.

Glennerster, H., Lupton, R., L., Noden, P. and Power, A. (1999). Poverty, Social Exclusion and Neighborhood: Studying the Area Bases of Social Exclusion. LSE STICERD Research Paper No. CASE022. Available at: SSRN: https://ssrn.com/abstract=1158913

Gore, C. and Figueiredo, J. B. (1997). *Social Exclusion and Anti-poverty Policy: A Debate*. Research Serious 110. Geneva: International Institute for Labour Studies, United Nations Development Programme.

Grech, A. (2014). Evaluating the Possible Impact of Pension Reform on Elderly Poverty in Europe. *Social Poverty & Administration*. ISSN: 0144-5596, DOI: 10.1111/spol.12084.

Grusky, D. B. (2001). Social stratification. In Smelser, N. J. and Baltes, P. B. (eds.). *International Encyclopedia of the Social & Behavioral Sciences*. Oxford, England: Elsevier.

Grusky, D. B. and Kanbur, R. (2006). Introduction: The Conceptual Foundations of Poverty and Inequality Measurement: 1-29. In Grusky, D. B., Kanbur, R. and Sen, A. K. (eds.). *Poverty and Inequality*, *Vol*, *Studies in Social Inequality*. Stanford, CA: Stanford University Press.

Guardiancich, I. (2010). *Denmark Current Pension System: First Assessment of Reform Outcomes and Output*. European Social Observatory, May 2010.

Gustafsson, B. and Uusitalo, H. (1990). Income Distribution and Redistribution During Two Decades—Experience from Finland and Sweden. *Generating Equality—The Swedish Experiment*. ed. I. Persson-Tanimura: 73-95. Oslo: Norwegian University Press.

Gustafsson, B., Johansson, M. and Palmer, E. (2009). The Welfare of Sweden's Old-age Pensioners in Times of Bust and Boom from 1990. *Ageing and Society*, 29(4): 539-561.

Hagen, K. and Kleinlein, A. (2012). *Ten years of the Riester pension scheme: no reason to celebrate*. DIW Economic Bulletin, 2: 2, 3—13, http//: www. diw. de/sixcms/detauk.php? id=diw_01.c.392365.de.

Haitz, N. (2015). Old-age Poverty in OECD Countries and the Issue of Gender Pension Gaps, *CESifo DICE Report*, 13 (2), 2015: 73-75.

Haan P., Stichnoth H., Blömer M., Buslei H. Geyer J., Krolage

C. and Müller K. (2017). Entwicklung der Altersarmut bis 2036, Trends, Risikogruppen und Politikszenarien. *Deutsch Institut für Wirtschaftsforschung (DIW) und dem Zentrum für Europäische Wirtschaftsforschung (ZEW)*. Bertelmann Stiftung.

Haughton, J. and Khandker, S. R. (2009). *Handbook of Poverty and Inequality*. Washington, DC: The World Bank.

HBAI Information Governance and Security Directorate Dept for Work and Pensions (2011/2012). *Changes to the Households Below Average Income*. United Kingdom.

Hedström, P. and Ringen, S. (1987). Age and income in contemporary society: A Research Note. *Journal of Social Policy*, *Volume* 16, Issue 2: 227-239.

Heinrich, G. A. (2000). *Affluence and Poverty in Old Age: New Evidence from the European Community Household Panel*. IRISS Working Paper Series 2000—2008, IRISS at CEPS/INSTEAD.

Hemerijck A. (2017). Changing Welfare States in Hard Times. *Oxford University Press*. London.

Herbermann, J. D. and Miranda, D. (2012). Defusing the demographic "time-bomb" in Germany. *Bull World Health Organ*, 90(1): 6-7.

Hewitt, C. (1977). The effect of political democracy and social democracy on equality in industrial societies. *American Sociological Review*, *Vol*, 42, No. 3: 450-464.

Hick, R. (2014). Poverty as Capability Deprivation: Conceptualizing and Measuring Poverty in Contemporary Europe. *European Journal of Sociology*, Vol. 55: 295-326.

Hill, K., Sutton, L. and Hirsch, D. (2011). *Living on a low income in later life*. London: Age UK, 69pp.

Hill, M. J. (1995). *Social Policy: A Comparative Analysis*. London: Prentice Hall/Harvester Wheatsheaf.

Hills, J. (1999). *Social Exclusion, Income Dynamics and Public Policy*. Sir Charles Carter lecture. (129). Northern Ireland Economic Council, Belfast, Northern Ireland. ISBN: 1897614519.

Hillyard, P., Lundström, F., Patsios, D., Machniewski, S., David Taylor, D. and Lyons, Maureen. (2010). *Inequalities in Old Age: An exploratory Study of the Impact of the Recession on Older People in Northern Ireland (NI) and the Republic of Ireland*. Centre for Ageing Research and Development in Ireland (CARDI): Belfast.

Hobson, B. (1994). Solo mothers, social policy regimes, and the logics of gender. in D. Sainsbury, D. (ed.). *Gendering Welfare States*. London: Sage.

Hoff, A. (2008). *Tackling Poverty and Social Exclusion of Older People—lessons From Europe*. Oxford institute of ageing. Oxford: University of Oxford.

International Labour Organization, World Social Protection Report. (2014/15). *Building Economic Recovery, Inclusive Development and Social Justice*. International Labour Office-Geneva: ILO, 2014. ISBN 978-92-2-128660-8.

Jäntti M. and Danziger, S. (2000). Income Poverty in Advanced Countries. in Anthony, B. A. and Bourguignon, F. (eds.). *Handbook of Income Distribution*, Vol. 1, 2000, Pages 309-378, North-Holland, Amsterdam.

Janoski, T. (1998). *Citizenship and Civil Society: A Framework of Rights and Obligation in Liberal, Traditional and Social Democratic Regimes*. Cambridge University Press, 1998.

Johnson, D. S. and Smeeding, T. M. (2012). A Consumer's Guide to Interpreting Various U. S. Poverty Measures. *Fast Focus, No*. 14-2013. Madison, WI: Institute for Research on Poverty.

Kaneff, D. and Pine, F. (2011). *Emerging Inequalities in Europe: Poverty and Transnational Migration*. Global Connections and Emerging Inequality in Europe: Perspectives on Poverty and Transnational Migration. Anthem Press, London, UK and New York, USA.

Kaneff, D. and Pine, F. (2011). *Global connections and emerging inequality in Europe: Perspectives on Poverty and Transnational Migration*. Anthem Press, London, UK, ISBN 9780857289698.

Kakwani, N. (1997). *Inequality, Welfare and Poverty: Three Interrelated Phenomena* (*Working paper* 97/18). Kensington, NSW: The University of New South Wales.

Kakwani, N. and Silber, J. (2007). *Many Dimensions of Poverty*. Basingstoke: Palsgrave Macmillan.

Kaneff, D. (2009). Property and Transnational Neoliberalism: The Case of British Migration to Bulgaria. In Valkanova, Y. (ed.). *Accession and migration: Changing policy, society and culture in an enlarged Europe*. Surrey: Ashgate, 59-74.

Kangas, O. and Ritakallio, V. M. (2008). *Köyhyyden mittaustavat, sosiaaliturvan riittävyys ja köyhyyden yleisyys Suomessa*. Sosiaali-ja terveysturvan selosteita 61/2008. Helsinki: Kelan tutkimusosasto.

Kautto, M. (2001). Diversity *Among Welfare States: Comparative Studies on Welfare State Adjustment in Nordic Countries*. Research Report 118, Saarijärvi: Stakes.

Kenworthy, L. (1999). Do Social-Welfare Policies Reduce Poverty? A Cross-National Assessment. *Social Forces*, Vol. 77, No. 3: 1119-1139.

Keyfitz, N. (1992). *Population Change and Social Policy*. Lanham: University Press of America.

Kidd, S. and Whitehouse, E. (2009). Pensions and Old-Age Poverty. In Holzmann, R., Robalino, D. A. and Takayama, N. (eds.). *Closing the Coverage Gap: The Role of Social Pensions and Other Retirement Income Transfers*. Washington, D. C.: World Bank: 41-55.

Kohli, M. (2007). The institutionalization of the life course: Looking back to look ahead. *Research in Human Development*, 4: 253-271. doi: 10.1080/15427600701663122.

Korpi, W. and Palme, J. (1998). The Paradox of Redistribution and Strategies of Equality: Welfare State Institutions, Inequality and Poverty in the Western Countries, *American Socioogical Review*, 63(5): 661-687.

Koutsampelas, C. (2012). Aspects of Elderly Poverty in Cyprus. *Cyprus Economic Policy Review*, Vol. 6, No. 1: 69-89.

Kröger, T. (2009). Care Research and Disability Studies: Nothing in Common? *Critical Social Policy*, 29 (3): 398-420.

Kröger, T. and Zechner, M. (2009). Migration and Care: Giving and Needing Care Across National Borders. *Finnish Journal of Ethnicity and Migration*, 4 (2): 17-26.

Kröger, T. and Leinonen, A. (2012). Transformation by Stealth: The Retargeting of Home Care Services in Finland. *Health and Social Care in the Community*, 20 (3), 319-327.

Kvist, J. (2014). *Pension, Health and Long-term Care Denmark*. Annual National Report, asisp country document update 2014 Denmark.

Lampman, R. (1964). The Problem of Poverty in America. *Economic Report of the President*, 1964, *U. S.* Government Printing Office. Washington, DC: 55-79.

Langan, M. and Ostner, I. (1991). Gender and welfare: towards a comparative framework. In Room, G. (ed.). *Towards a European Welfare State*. Bristol: SAUS Publications.

Laursen, T., Andersen, T. M. and Jahn Detlef. (2016). *Sustainable Governance Indicators*. 2015 Denmark Report.

Laursen F., Andersen M. T. and Jahn D. (2017). Denmark Report. Sustainable Governance Indicators 2017. *Bertelsmann Stiftung*.

Lee, C. and Koo, I. (2017). The welfare states and poverty. *The Oxford Handbook of the Social Science of Poverty*. Oxford Handbooks Online, DOI: 10.1093/oxfordhb/9780199914050.013.32.

Ledeneva, A. (1998). *Russia's Economy of Favours: Blat, Networking and Informal Exchange*. Cambridge: Cambridge University Press.

Leibfried, S. (1992). Towards a European welfare state? On Integrating Poverty Regimes into the European Community. In Ferge, Z. and Kolberg, J. E. (eds.). *Social Policy in a Changing Europe*. Frankfurt am Main: Campus Verlag.

Leichsenring K., Billings J., Nies H. (2013). *Long-term care in Europe, improving policy and practice*. Palgrave Macmillan UK.

Leisering, L. (2003). Government and the Life Course. In DeLamater, J. (ed.). *Handbook of Sociology and Social Research*. Springer US, ISSN: 1389-6903.

Leisering, L. and Leibfried, S. (2001). Paths out of Poverty: Perspectives on Active Policy. In Giddens, A. (ed.). *The Global Third Way Debate*. Cambridge: Polity Press.

Lelkes, O. and Gasior, K. (2012). *Income Poverty and Social Exclusion in the EU: Situation in 2008 and Trends (based on EU-SILC 2005—2009)*. European Centre for social welfare policy and research. Policy Brief.

Lelkes, O., Medgyesi, M. and Tóth G. I. (2009). The Factors Affecting the Risk of Poverty and Inequalities in Income Distribution. In Ward, T., Lelkes, O., Sutherland, H. and Tóth G. I. (eds.). *European inequalities: social inclusion and income distribution in the European Union*. Budapest. ISBN 978-963-7869-40-2.

Lemke, T. P. and Lins, G. T. (2013). *ERISA for Money Managers 2013 ed*. Legal Works.

Levy, R. and Bühlmann, F. (2016). Towards A Socio-structural Framework for Life Course Analysis. *Advances in Life Course Research*, Vol. 30: 30-42.

Lewis, J. (1992). Gender and the development of welfare regimes, *Journal of European Social Policy*, Vol. 2, Issue 3.

Lewis, J. and Ostner, I. (1995). Gender and the evolution of European social policy. In Leibfreid, S. and Pierson, P. (eds.). *European Social Policy*. Washington, DC: Brookings Institute.

Maisonneuve, C. and Martins, J. O. (2013). *Public Spending on Health and Long-term Care: A New Set of Projections*. OECD Economic Policy papers, No. 6. ISSN: 2226583X.

Mantovani, D., Papadopoulos, F., Sutherland, H. and Tsakloglou, P. (2005). *Pension Incomes in the European Union: Policy Reform Strategies in Comparative Perspective*. IZA Discussion Paper, No. 1537.

Mares, I. and Carnes, M. E. (2009). Social policy in developing countries. *Annual Review of Political Science*, Vol. 12: 93-113.

Marlier, E., Atkinson, A. B., Cantillon, B. and Nolan, B. (2007). *The EU and Social Inclusion: Facing the Challenges*. Bristol: The Policy Press.

Marx, I. and Nelson, K. (2013). *Minimum Income Protection in Flux*. Basingstoke: Palgrave Macmillan UK.

Mayer, K. U. (2005). Life courses and life chances in a comparative perspective. In S. Svallfors, S. (ed.). *Analyzing Inequality: Life Chances and Social Mobility in Comparative Perspective*. CA: Stanford University Press: 17-55.

Mayer, K. U. (2009). New directions in life course research. *Annual Review of Sociology*, Vol. 35: 413-433. doi: 10.1146/annurev.soc.34.040507.134619.

Mathew, P. J., Kröger, T. and Van Aerschot, L. (2015). Users of home-care services in a Nordic welfare state under marketisation: The rich, the poor and the sick. *Health and Social Care in the Community*, 25(1): 54-64. DOI: 10.1111/hsc.12245.

McKernan, S. M. and Ratcliffe, C. (2006). The Effect of Specific Welfare Policies on Poverty. The Urban Institute, April 2006. Available at SSRN: https://ssrn.com/abstract=2205845 or http://dx.doi.org/10.2139/ssrn.2205845

Meagher, G. and Szebehely, M. (2013a). Long-term care in Sweden: trends, actors and consequences. In Ranci, C. and Pavolini, E. (eds.). *Reforms in Long Term Care Policies in Europe: Investigating Institutional Change and Social Impacts*. New York: Springer.

Meagher, G. and Szebehely, M. (eds.). (2013b). *Marketisation in Nordic Eldercare: A Research Report on Legislation, Oversight, Extent and Consequences*. Stockholm University: Department of Social Work.

Minkler, M. and Estes, C. L. (1991). *Critical Perspectives on Aging: The Political and Moral Economy of Growing Old*. Routledge, 1 edition.

MISSOC. (2000). Germany: Old-age, European Commission.

Ministry of Social Welfare & Ministry of Health and Prevention. (2008). Denmark National Report on Strategies for Social Protection and Social Inclusion 2008—2010.

Ministry of Social Affairs and Integration. (2011). Social Policy in Denmark. Danish *Presidency of the Council of the European Union*. Holmens Kanal, København K.

Moser, C. O. N. (1998). The Asset Vulnerability Framework: Reassessing Urban Poverty Reduction Strategies. *World Development*, Vol. 26, Issue 1: 1-19.

Motel-Klingebiel, A. (2004). Quality of Life and Social Inequality in Old Age. In Daatland, S. O. and Biggs, S. (eds.). *Ageing and Diversity: Multiple Pathways in Later Life*. Bristol: Policy Press: 189-205.

Motel-Klingebiel, A. and Gilberg, R. (2002). Zielsetzungen, Perspektiven und Probleme bei Surveybefragungen mit alten Menschen. In Motel-Klingebiel, A. and Kelle, U. (eds.). *Perspektiven der Empirischen Alter(n)ssoziologie*. Opladen, Lese and Budrich: 133-153.

Naegele, G. and Schnabel, E. (2010). *Measures for Social Inclusion of Older People: The Case of Volunteering*. Working Paper, European Foundation for the Improvement of Living and Working Conditions.

Narayan, D., Patel, R., Schafft, K., Rademacherand, A. and Koch-Schultz, S. (2000). *Voices of the Poor. Can Anyone Hear Us?* Oxford: Oxford University Press (for the World Bank).

Nelson, K. (2012). Counteracting material deprivation: The role of social assistance in Europe. *Journal of European Social Policy*, 22(2): 148-163.

Nygård, M., Härtull, C., Wentjärvi, A. and Jungerstam, S.

(2016). Poverty and Old Age in Scandinavia: A Problem of Gendered Injustice? Evidence from the 2010 GERDA Survey in Finland and Sweden. *Social Indicator Research*, Vol. 132, Issue 2: 681-698.

OECD. (2011). *Help Wanted? Providing and Paying for Long-Term Care*. ISBN: 978-92-64-097582. Available at: https://www.oecd.org/els/health-systems/47903344.pdf.

OECD. (2014). *Society at a Glance* 2014 *Highlights: Denmark*. OECD social indicators. Available at: http://www.oecd.org/denmark/OECD-SocietyAtaGlance2014-Highlights-Denmark.pdf.

OECD. (2014). *Society at a Glance* 2014 *Highlights: Germany*. OECD social indicators. Available at: http://www.oecd.org/germany/OECD-SocietyAtaGlance2014-Highlights-Germany.pdf.

OECD. (2014). *Society at a Glance* 2014 *Highlights: United Kingdom*. OECD social indicators. Available at: https://www.oecd.org/unitedkingdom/OECD-SocietyAtaGlance2014-Highlights-UnitedKingdom.pdf.

OECD. (2016). *Society at a Glance* 2016: *OECD Social Indicators*. OECD Publishing, Paris. http://dx.doi.org/10.1787/9789264261488-en.

OECD. (2017). *Society at a Glance* 2017: *OECD and G20 Indicators*. Country profile, Germany.

OECD. (2017). *Society at a Glance* 2017: *How does Germany Compare?*

OECD. (2017). *Society at a Glance* 2017: *OECD and G20 Indicators*.

Office for National Statistics. (2012). *Comparison of UK and EU at-risk-of-poverty rates*, 2005—2010. Available at: http://webarchive.nationalarchives.gov.uk/20160114000937/

http://www.ons.gov.uk/ons/dcp171776_266844.pdf.

OECD Health Policy Studies. (2011). *Help Wanted? Providing and Paying for Long-Term Care*. Organization for Economic Co-Operation & Development.

Office for national statistics. (2014). Persistent Poverty in the UK and EU: rates of persistent relative income poverty for the UK are compared with EU countries. Available at: https://www.ons.gov.uk/peoplepopulationandcommunity/personalandhouseholdfinances/incomeandwealth/articles/persistentpovertyintheukandeu/2014.

O'Higgins, M. (1985). Inequality, redistribution and recession: the British experience, 1976—1982. *Journal of Social Policy*, Vol. 14, Issue 3.

Oris, M. and Lerch, M. (2009). La transition ultime. Longévitéet mortalitéaux grands âges dans le bassin lémanique (The last transition. Longevity and mortality at old age in the Lemanic area). In Oris, M., Widmer, E., De Ribaupierre, A., Joye, D., Spini, D., Labouvie-Vief, G. and Falter, J. M. (eds.). *Transitions dans le parcours de vie et construction des inégalités (Transitions in the life course and the construction of inequalities)*. Lausanne, Switzerland: Presses polytechniques et universitaires romandes.

Oris, M., Dubert, I., and Viret, J. L. (2015). Vieillir: Les apports de la démographie historique et de l'histoire de la famille (Aging: The contributions of historical demography and family history). *Annales De Démographie Historique*, 129: 201-229. doi: 10.3917/adh.129.0201.

Oris, M., Guichard, E., Nicolet, M., Gabriel, R., Tholomier, A., Monnot, C., Fagot, D. and Joye, D. (2016). Representation of vulnerability and older people. A total survey error perspective on the VLV survey. In Oris, M., Roberts, C., Joye, D. and Staähl, M. E. (eds.). *Surveying human vulnerabilities across the life course*: 27-64. Heidelberg, Germany: Springer.

Oris, M., Gabriel, R., Ritschard, G. and Kliegel, M. (2017). Long lives and old age poverty social stratification and life course institutionalization in Switzerland. *Research in Human Development*, Vol. 14, Issue 1: 68-87.

Oris, M., Roberts, C., Joye, D. and Stähl, E. M. (2016). Surveying Human Vulnerabilities Across the Life Course: Balancing Substantive and Methodological Challenges. *Life Course Research and Social Policies book series*, Vol. 3: 1-25. Online available: https://link.springer.com/chapter/10.1007/978-3-319-24157-9_1/fulltext.html.

Orshansky, M. (1965). Counting the Poor: Another Look at the Poverty Profile. *Social Security Bulletin*, Vol. 28(1): 3-29.

Orshansky, M. (1965). Counting the Poor: Another Look at the Poverty Profile. *Social Security Bulletin*, Vol. 28(1): 3-29.

Palier B. (2010). A Long Goodbye to Bismarck? The Politics of Welfare Reforms in Continental Europe. *Amsterdam University Press*. Amsterdam.

Paugman, S. (1991). *La Disqualification Sociale. Essai Sur La Nouvelle Pauvreté*. Paris: Presses Universitaires de France, 1991.

Pawlik, W. (1992). Intimate Commerce. In Wdel, J. ed. *The Unplanned Society: Poland during and after Communism*. New York: Columbia University Press.

Petra, E. T. and Clement, J. (2011). *How the Design of a Pension System Influences Old Age Poverty and Gender Equity: A Study of Chile's Private Retirement Accounts System*. Paper presented at the LACEA meetings in Santiago, Chile, Nov., 2011.

Pfau-Effinger, B. , Eichler, M. and Och, R. (2012), Erklärung der Differenzen in der lokalen Sozialpolitik zur Pflegélterer Menschen in West-und Ostdeutschland. In Soeffner, Georg; Kursawe, Kathy (Hg). *Transnationale Vergesellschaftungen : Verhandlungen des* 35. Kongresses der Deutschen Gesellschaft für Soziologie in Frankfurt am Main 2010. Wiesbaden: VS Verlag.

Pfau-Effinger, B. , Flaquer, L. , Jensen, P. H. (2009). *Formal and Informal Work in Europe*. The Hidden Work Regime. London, New York: Routledge

Pfau-Effinger, B. , Jensen, P. H, Och, R. (2011). Tension between "Consumerism" in Elderly Care and the Social Right of Family Carers: a German-Danish Comparison. *Nordic Journal for Social Research*, Vol. 2: 7-22.

Phillipson, C. (1981). Women in later life: pattern of control and subordination, In Hutter, B. and Williams, G. (eds.). *Controlling Women: The Normal and the Deviant*. London: Croom Helm.

Piachaud, D. (1987). Problems in the Definition and Measurement of Poverty, *Journal of Social Policy*, Vol. 16, Issue 2: 147-164.

Pine, F. (2002). Retreat to The Household? Gendered Domains in Postsocialist Poland. In Hann, C. M. ed. *Postsocialism: Ideals, Ideologies and Practices in Eurasia*. London: Routledge

Polin, V. and Raitano, M. (2012). *Poverty Dynamics in Clusters of European Union Countries: Related Events and Main Determinants*. Available at SSRN: https://ssrn.com/abstract=2025018 or http://dx.doi.org/10.2139/ssrn.2025018

Ravallion, M. (2011). On Multidimensional Indices of Poverty. *Journal of Economic Inequality*, Vol. 9, Issue 2: 235-248.

Ravallion, M. (2014a). The Idea of Antipoverty Policy. In Atkinson, A. B. and Bourguignon, F. (eds.). *Handbook of Income Distribution*. New York: Elsevier-North-Holland.

Ravallion, M. (2014b). Income Inequality in the Developing World. *Science*, Vol. 344, Issue 6186: 815-855.

Ravallion, M. and Chen, S. (1996). Data in Transition: Assessing Rural Living Standards in Southern China, *China Economic Review*, Vol. 7, Issue 1: 23-55.

Ravallion, M. and Chen, S. (2011). Developing World is Poorer than We Thought, but No Less Successful in the Fight Against Poverty. *Quarterly Journal of Economics*, Vol. 125, Issue 4: 1577-1625.

Ravallion, M., Chen, S. and Sangraula, P. (2009). Dollar a Day Revisited. *World Bank Economic Review*, Vol. 23, No. 2: 163-184.

Ravallion, M., Datt, G. and van de Walle, D. (1991). Quantifying Absolute Poverty in the Developing World. *Review of Income and Wealth*, Vol. 37: 345-361.

Ravallion, M., Datt, G. and van de Walle, D. (1991). The Impact of Food Pricing Reforms on Poverty: A Demand Consistent Welfare Analysis for Indonesia. *Journal of Policy Modeling*, Vol. 13: 281-300.

Riedmüller, B. and Willert, M. (2007). The German pension system and social inclusion. In Meyer, T., Bridgen, P. and Riedmüller, B. (eds.). *Private pension versus Social Inclusion? Non-state Provision for Citizens at Risk in Europe*. Cheltenham: Edward Elgar: 139-167.

Ringen, S. (1985). Toward a Third Stage in the Measurement of Poverty. *Act Fociologica*, Vol. 28, No. 2: 99-113.

Ringen, S. (1987). *The Politics of Possibility: a Study in the Political*

Economy of the Welfare State. Oxford: Clarendon Press.

Ringen, S. and Uusitalo, H. (1990). Income distribution and redistribution in the Nordic Welfare states. In Kolberg, J. E. (ed.). *Comparing Welfare States and Labor Markets: The Scandinavian Model*. Armonk, NY: M. E. Sharpe.

Rodrigues, C. F. and Andrade, I. (2013). *The Old Age Problem of Old Age Poverty in Portugal*. School of Economics and Management, the Centre for Applied Mathematics and Economics. Working Paper, ISSN: 0874-4548.

Room, G. J. (1999). Social Exclusion, Solidarity and the Challenge of Globalization. *International Journal of Social Welfare*, Vol. 8, Issue 3: 166-174.

Rooney, T. and Great Britain Parliament House of Commons: Work and Pensions Committee. (2009). *Tackling pensioner poverty: fifth report of session* 2008—2009, Vol. 2. The Stationery Office.

Rothgang, H. (2010). Social Insurance for Long-term Care: an evaluation of the German model, social insurance for long-term care. *Social Policy and Administration*, Vol. 44, Issue 4: 436-460.

Rowntree, B. S. (1901). *Poverty, A Study of Town Life*. London: Macmillan and Co, UK.

Sainsbury, D. (1994). *Gendering Welfare States*. London: Sage.

Sainsbury, D. (1999). Gender, policy regimes and politics. In Sainsbury, D. (ed.). *Gender and Welfare State Regimes*. Oxford: Oxford University Press.

Saltman, R. B., Dubois, H. F. and Chawla, M. (2006). The impact of aging on long-term care in Europe and some potential policy responses, *International Journal of Health Services*, Vol. 36, Issue 4: 719-746.

Sawyer, M. (1982). Income distribution and the welfare state. In Boetho, A. (ed.). *The European Economy*. Oxford: Oxford University Press.

Schmähl, W. (2007). Dismantling an earnings-related social pension scheme: Germany's new pension policy, *Journal of Social Policy*, Vol. 36, Issue 2: 319-340.

Schröder-Butterfill, E., and Marianti, R. (2006). A framework for understanding old-age vulnerabilities. *Ageing and Society*, 26 (1): 9-35.

Schut, J. M. W., Vrooman, J. C., and de Beer, P. T. (2001). *On Worlds of Welfare. Institutions and Their Effects in Eleven Welfare States*. The Hague: Social and Cultural Planning Office, April 2001.

Sen, A. K. (1976). Poverty: An Ordinal Approach to Measurement. *Econometrica*, Vol. 44, Issue 2: 219-231.

Sen, A. K. (1980). Equality of what? In McMurrin, S. (ed.). *Tanner Lectures on Human Values*. Cambridge: Cambridge University Press.

Sen, A. K. (1985). A Sociological Approach to the Measurement of Poverty: A Reply to Professor Peter Townsend. *Oxford Economic Papers*, Vol. 37, No. 4: 669-676.

Sen, A. K. (1992). *Inequality Reexamined*. Cambridge, MA: Harvard University Press.

Sen, A. K. (1999). *Development as Freedom*. New York: Anchor Books.

Shepherd, A., Scott, L. Mariotti, C., Kessy, F., Gaiha, R., da Corta, L., Hanifnia, K., Kaicker, N., Lenhardt, A., Lwanga-Ntale, C., Sen, B., Sijapati, B., Strawson, Tim., Thapa, G., Underhill, H. and Wild, L. (2014). *The Chronic Poverty Report* 2014—2015: *The road to zero extreme pov-*

erty. Overseas Development Institute, London.

Siaoff, A. (1994). Work, Welfare and Gender Equality: a New Typology. In Sainsbury, D. (ed.). *Gendering Welfare States*. London: Sage.

Smeeding T. (2015). "Poverty, sociology of," in *International Encyclopedia of the Social & Behavioral Sciences* ed. Wright J. D., editor. (Oxford: Elsevier) 753-759. 10.1016/b978-0-08-097086-8.32113-4.

Smeeding, T. M. (2016). *The Oxford Handbook of The Social Science of Poverty: Poverty Measurement*. Oxford University Press, Sheridan, USA.

Smeeding, T. M. (2006). Poor People in Rich Nations: The United States in Comparative Perspective. *Journal of Economic Perspectives*, Vol. 20, No. 1: 69-90.

Smeeding, T. M. and Sandstrom, S. (2004). *Poverty and Income Maintenance Old Age: A Cross-national View of Low Income Older Women*. Center for Retirement Research at Boston College.

Smeeding, T. M., Torrey, B., and Rein, M. (1988). Patterns of income and poverty: the economic status of children and older people in eight countries. In Palmer, J., Smeeding, T. M. and Torrey, B. (eds.). *The Vulnerable*. Washington, DC: The Urban Institute Press.

Speer, J. W. (2017). *When does Medicaid Pay for Long-term care?* Published on Senior Navigator: https://seniornavigator.org/article/62307/when-does-medicaid-pay-long-term-care-revised-2017

Social Protection Committee and the European Commission. (2014). *Adequate Social Protection for Long-term Care Needs in an Ageing Society*. Report jointly prepared by the. Publications Office of the European Union, Luxembourg.

Social Protection Committee (SPC) and the European Commission (DG EMPL). (2015). *Pension Adequacy Report: Current and Future Income Adequacy in Old Aage in EU*. Publications Office of the European Union, Luxembourg. ISBN 978-92-79-51683-2.

Social Security Programs Throughout the World. (2016). Europe, 2016, Germany: 119-126. Available at: https://www.ssa.gov/policy/docs/progdesc/ssptw/2016-2017/europe/germany.pdf

Spicker, P., Leguizamon, S. A., Gordon, D., Comparative Research Programme on Poverty., and International Social Science Council. (2007). *Poverty: An International Glossary*. London: Zed Books.

Spini, D., Bernardi, L. and Oris, M. (2017). Vulnerability Across the Life Course, *Research in Human Development*, Vol. 14, Issue 1: 1-4, DOI: 10.1080/15427609.2016.1268891.

Statisticishes Bundesamt. (2003). 2. Bericht: Pflegestatistik 2001. Pflege im Rahmen der Pflegeversicherung. Ländervergleich Pflegebedürftige, Bonn. Available at: https://www.destatis.de/DE/Publikationen/Thematisch/Soziales/Sozialpflege2Bericht2001.pdf?blob=publicationFile

Statisticishes Bundesamt. (2013). Pflegestatistik 2011. Pflege im Rahmen der Pflegeversicherung. Ländervergleich Pflegebedürftige, Wiesbaden. Available at: https://www.destatis.de/DE/Publikationen/Thematisch/Gesundheit/Pflege/LaenderPflegebeduerftige5224002119004.pdf?blob=publicationFile

Statisticishes Bundesamt. (2017). Pflegestatistik 2015. Pflege im Rahmen der Pflegeversicherung Deutschlandergebnisse,

Wiesbaden. Available at: https://www.destatis.de/DE/Publikationen/Thematisch/Gesundheit/Pflege/PflegeDeutschlandergebnisse5224001159004.pdf?blob=publicationFile

Statistic Denmark. (2018). Documentation of Statistics for Old Age Pension and Disability Pension, Sejrøgade 11DK 2100 København K.

Stephen, J. (1979). *The Transition from Capitalism to Socialism*. London: Macmillan.

Summers, R. and Heston, A. (1988). New Set of International Comparisons of Real Product and Price Levels: Estimates for 130 Countries, 1950—1985. *Review of Income and Wealth*, Series 34, No. 1 (March, 1988): 1-25, and three accompanying computer diskettes.

Swift, J. (1989). Why Are Rural People Vulnerable to Faminé *IDS Bulletin*, Vol. 20, No. 2: 8-15.

Szebehely, M. (2013). *Individualised care and universal welfare: Dilemmas in an era of marketisation*. Swedish Research Council for Health, Working Life and Welfare. Stockholm University, Sweden.

The Directorate-General for Employment, Social Affairs and Inclusion of the European Commission and the Social Protection Committee. (2012). *Pension Adequacy in the European Union* 2010—2050. ISBN: 978-92-79-25951-7.

The Ministry of Social Affairs and Integration. (2015). *Social policy in Denmark*. ISBN: 978-87-7546-281-0. Available at: http://www.oim.dk/media/14947/social-policy-in-denmark.pdf.

Theobald, H. and Hampel, S. (2013). Radical Institutional Change and Incremental Transformation: Long-Term Care Insurance in Germany. In Ranci, C. and Pavolini,

E. (eds.). *Reforms in Long-Term Care Policies in Europe: Investigating Institutional Change and Social Impacts*. New York, NZ: Springer, 117-138.

The OECD Health Project. (2005). *Long-term care for Older People*. ISSN: 19901291. (online) http://dx.doi.org/10.1787/19901291.

Tinson, A., Ayrton, C., Karen, B., Born, T. B., Aldridge, H. and Kenway, P. (2016). *Monitoring Poverty and Social Exclusion* 2016. York: Joseph Rowntree Foundation.

Torp, C. (2015). *Challenge of Aging: Pensions, Retirement and Generational Justice*. Oundmills, Basingstoke, Hampshire; New York, NY: Palgrave Macmillan.

Townsend, P. (1979). *Poverty in the United Kingdom: A Survey of Household Resources and Standards of Living*. Penguin Books Ltd. New York.

Twigg, J. (2013). *Fashion and Age, Dress, the Body and Later Life*. London: Bloomsbury Academic, Great Britain.

United Nations Research Institute for Social Development. (2010). Combating Poverty and Inequality: Structural Change, Social Policy and Politics. Geneva: UNRISD Flagship Report. ISBN: 978-92-9085-076-2.

Ungerson, C. (2004). Whose Empowerment and Independence? A cross-national perspective on "cash for care" scheme. *Aging & Society*, Vol. 24, Issue 2: 189-212.

Ungerson, C. (2005). Care, work and feeling. *The Sociological Review*, Vol. 53, Issue 2: 188-203.

Van Mechelen, N., Marchal, S., Goedemé, T., Marx, I. and Cantillon, B. (2011). *The CSB Minimum Income Protection Indicators Dataset* (*CSB-MIPI*) (No. WP No. 11/05). Antwerp: Herman Deleeck Centre for Social Policy.

Vampa, D. (2017). From National to Sub-national? Exploring the Territorial Dimension of Social Assistance in Italy. *Journal of Social Policy*, Vol. 46, Issue 2: 269-289.

Vidje, G. (2013). *The Nordic Welfare Model*. Nordic Centre for Welfare and Social Issues. Stockholm, Sweden. ISBN: 978-87-7919-078-8.

Villar, A. (2016). Educational Poverty as A Welfare Loss: Low Performance in The OECD According to PISA 2012. *Modern Economy*, Vol. 7: 441-449. doi: 10. 4236/me. 2016.74049.

Villar, A. (2017). *Lectures on Inequality, Poverty and Welfare*. Springer International Publishing. Switzerland.

Waglé, U. R. (2008). Multidimensional Poverty: An Alternative Measurement Approach for the United States. *Social Science Research*, Vol. 37, Issue 2: 559-580.

Waldhausen, A. (2014). *Care Services in Crisis? Long-term Care in Times of European Economic and Financial Crisis*. Frankfurt am Main: Institute for Social Work and Social Education.

Walker, A. (1981). Towards a political economy of old age. *Ageing and Society*, Vol. 1, Issue 1: 73-94. doi: 10.1017/S0144686X81000056.

Walker, A., Maltby, T. and Walker, C. (1997). *Altenhilfe in Europa: Länderbericht Vereinigtes Königreich, in BMFSFJ (ed.). Altenhilf in Europa, Länderberichte: Dänemark, Niederlande, Vereinigtes Königreich, Frankreich, Spanien*. Stuttgart: Kohlhammer: 196-323.

Walker, R., Heaver, C. and McKay, S. (2000). *Building up pension rights*. DWP Research Report No. 114. London: Department for Work and Pensions.

Whelan, C. T., Brian Nolan, B. and Maître, B. (2014). Multidimensional Poverty Measurement in Europe：An Application of the Adjusted Headcount Approach. *Journal of European Social Policy*, Vol. 24(2)：183-197.

Whelan, C. T., Nolan, B. and Bertrand, M. (2007). Consistent Poverty and Economic Vulnerability (Dublin, Institute of Public Administration). In Fahey, T., Russell, H and Whelan, C. T. (eds.). *Quality of Life in Ireland：Social Impact of Economic Boom*. Springer.

Whelan, C. T., Nolan, B. and Bertrand, M. (2014). Multidimensional Poverty Measurement in Europe：An Application of the Adjusted Headcount Approach. *Journal of European Social Policy*, Vol. 24, Issue 2：183-197.

Willert, M. (2011). Consistent Poverty and Economic Vulnerability (Dublin, Institute of Public Administration) Consistent Poverty and Economic Vulnerability. In Clasen, J. (ed.). *Converging Worlds of Welfare? Britain and German Social Policy in the 21st Century*. Oxford：Oxford University Press：218-44.

Wimer C. T., Liana, F., Irv, G., Neeraj, K. and Waldfogel, J. (2013). *Trends in Poverty with an Anchored Supplemental Poverty Measure*. Institute for Research on Poverty Discussion Paper No. 1416—13. New York：Columbia Population Research Center.

Wood, G. and Gough, I. (2006). A comparative welfare regime approach to global social policy. *World Development*, Vol. 34, Issue 10：1696-1712.

Woolard, I., Harttgen, K. and Klasen, S. (2010). *The Evolution and Impact of Social Security in South Africa*. Paper prepared as a background paper for the conference on "Promoting Resilience trough Social Protection in Sub-Saharan African",

Dakar 28-30 June, last accessed on 3 March 2012.

World Social Security Report. (2010/2011). *Coverage by Social Security Pensions: Income Security in Old Age*. International Labor Organization. ISBN: 9789221292012.

World Social Security Report. (2014/2015). *Building Economic Recovery, Inclusive Development and Social Justice*. International Labor Organization. ISBN 978-92-2-128660-8.

Yates, S. J. (2004). *Living with Poverty in Post-Soviet Russia: Social Perspective on Urban Poverty*. Ph. D Dissertation, London School of Economic and Political Science.

Zaidi, A. (2006). Poverty of Elderly People in EU25. *Policy Brief* 8/2006. Vienna: European Centre.

Zaidi, A. (2008). *Well-being of Older People in Ageing Societies*. Aldershot: Ashgate Publishing Limited.

Zaidi, A. (2010). Poverty Risks for Older People in EU Countries-An Update. *Policy Brief* 1/2010. Vienna: European Centre.

Zaidi, A. and Gustafsson, B. (2006). *Work History, Retirement Choices and Incomes in Old Age: A Case Study of Sweden*. Submitted Papers Session 2D, "Aging, Intergenerational Transfers, and the Well-being of older people," At International Association for Research in Income and Wealth conference, Joensuu, Finland, 20-26, August.

Zaidi, A. and de Vos, K. (2008). Income Mobility of older people in Great Britain and thc Netherlands: A Comparative Investigation. In Zaidi, A. (ed.). *Well-being of Older People in Ageing Societies*. Aldershot: Ashgate Publishing Limited.

Zaidi, A., Gasior, K., Hofmarcher, M. M., Lelkes, O., Marin, B., Rodrigues, R., Schmidt, A., Vanhuysse, P. and Zolyomi, E. (2013). *Active Ageing Index 2012: Concept,*

Methodology and Final Results. Methodology report submitted to the European Commission's DG Employment, Social Affairs and Inclusion, and to the Population Unit, United Nations Economic Commission for Europe, for the project "Active Ageing Index (AAI)". UNECE Grant No: ECE/GC/2012/003. Vienna: European Centre for Social Welfare Policy and Research.

Zaidi, A. Grech, A. G. and Fuchs, M. (2006). *Pension Policy in EU25 and Its Possible Impact on Elderly Poverty*. CASE/116. Centre for Analysis of Social Exclusion, London School of Economics and Political Science, London, UK.

Zaidi, A., Gasior, K. and Zólyomi, E. (2010). Poverty amongst older Women and pensions policy in the European union. In Marin, B. and Zólyomi, E. (eds.). *Women's Work and Pensions: What is Good, What is Best? Designing Gender-Sensitive Arrangements*. Routledge.

Žilová, A., Novená, A., Joseph, M. V. et al. (2014). *European and Global Context of Poverty. Educatt, Milan, Italy*. ISBN: 978-88-6780-072-8.

Zaidi, A., Rake, K. and Falkingham, J. (2008). Income mobility in old age. In Zaidi, A. (ed.). *Well-being of Older People in Ageing Societies*. Aldershot: Ashgate Publishing Limited.

Appendix

Appendix 1: Theoretical typology of Germany, Denmark and UK-ideal models—on ageing policy's impact in preventing poverty risk for older people

Table 1: Theoretical typology of different types of ageing policy—the ideal models			
Dimensions	Typology of different types of ageing policy model (Ageing policy's impact on poverty risk)	Generosity level of ageing policy	Country examples
A: Eligibility requirements before an individual access to benefits	Not all policy fields help to avoid poverty risk for older people and they partly affect each other	Poverty less protected model	The UK
	All policy fields help to avoid poverty risk for older people	Poverty more protected model	Denmark
B: Size of benefit in the degree to which individual could access	All ageing policy fields may contribute to the poverty risk for older people and incompletely compensate with each other	Poverty medium level	Germany

Source: this table was created by the author, note: Germany, Denmark and UK are country samples in this dissertation.

Appendix 2: Assessment measures with criteria, Germany long-term care insurance

Table 2: assessment measures with criteria, Germany long-term care insurance		
measurement areas	degree	scoring points
mobility	10%	12.5～27
cognitive and communication skills	15%	27～47.5
behavior and psychological problems		
self-care	40%	47.5～70
ability to cope with and independent handling of demands and pressures caused by illness or the need for therapy	20%	70～90
organizing everyday life and social contacts	15%	90～100

Source: das Zweites Pflegestärkungsgesetz, 2018

Appendix 3: German long-term—Home care benefits, 2018

Table 3: German Long-term care Home care (€/monthly), 2017		
care grades	Cash benefits for care at home (low level, pay to care receivers not care giver)	In-kind benefits for care at home (long-term care insurance covered)
CG1	125	
CG2	316	689
CG3	545	1298
CG4	728	1612
CG5	901	1995

* As a sum of money that is available to pay for custodial care and caregiver relief benefits

Source: das Zweites Pflegestärkungsgesetz, 2018.

Appendix 4: German long-term care Residential care benefits, 2018

Table 4: German long-term care Residential care (€/monthly), 2017		
care grades	care payment	additional support
CG1	125	basic amount €104/increased amount €208
CG2	770	
CG3	1,262	
CG4	1,775	
CG5	2,005	—

Source: das Zweites Pflegestärkungsgesetz, 2018.

Appendix 5: UK care benefit with allowance

Table 5: the UK care benefit with allowance		
Attendance allowance (£/a week)	Personal allowance paid to couple pensioners (£/a week)	Carer's allowance (£/a week)
57.30 lower rate 85.65 higher rate	128.40	62.70

Source: United Kingdom Public Sector Information, 2016. https://www.gov.uk/carers-allowance, https://www.gov.uk/attendance-allowance, https://www.gov.uk/guidance/adjusted-net-income

Acknowledgement

After an intensive period, today is the day and this dissertation has been finished. Writing this note of thanks is the finishing touch to my dissertation. It has been a period of intense learning for me, not only in the scientific arena, but also on a personal level. Writing this dissertation has had a big impact on me. I would like to reflect on the people who have supported and helped me so much throughout this period.

I would particularly like to single out my supervisor Prof. Dr. Birgit Pfau-Effinger, I want to thank her for her excellent guidance, patience and for all of the opportunities I was given to conduct my research and further my dissertation, and most importantly, for her friendship during my studies at the University of Hamburg. Her mentorship was paramount in providing a well-rounded experience consistent with my long-term career goals. She encouraged me to not only grow as a scholar and a scientist, but also as an independent thinker. I am sure that many doctoral students are given the opportunity to develop their own individuality and self-sufficiency by being allowed to work with such independence. For everything she has done for me, I thank her.

I would also like to thank all of the members of the chair team, especially Thurid Eggers, for her valuable suggestions on tables in the dissertation and translation of the abstract, Ralf Och and Thordis Reimer for offering suggestions on dissertation procedure. These friends also provided me with some much-needed humor and entertainment in what could have otherwise been a somewhat stressful research environment.

I would also like to thank Prof. Rolf von Lüde as my second supervisor for his assistance and guidance in getting my career started on the right foot and having the patience to answer my questions and read my research reports. In the long run, I believe that his actions provided me with the unique opportunity to gain a wider insight into doing academic research.

I would like to thank the Faculty of Business, Economics and Social Sciences at the University of Hamburg, especially those members of my doctoral committee for their input, valuable discussions and accessibility. And I thank to the Chinese Scholarship Council for financial support to all these years of my Ph. D study. Also, I am grateful for the support and financial support from our graduate school to help me to present this dissertation at many international academic conferences and gain valuable feedback.

In particular, I would like to thank my friends Jia Wang, Chengcheng, Chen Wang and Meike for their emotional supports, patience and friendship, which has helped to reduce my stress, and for sharing wonderful moments in all these years in Hamburg.

Finally, and most importantly, I would like to thank my husband for his support, encouragement, quiet patience, and unwavering love were undeniably the bedrock upon which the past eight years of my life have been built. His tolerance of my occasional bad moods is a testament in itself to his unyielding devotion and love. His support by taking care of me and our young child while I was working on academic research is the strongest force behind me. I thank my parents for their faith in me and allowing me to be as ambitious as I wanted. It was under their watchful eye that I gained so much drive and an ability to tackle challenges head on. Also, I thank my parents-in-law. They provided us with great support through their unending encouragement, helping us through a happy and emotional period when my son was born.